Birchsong
Poetry Centered in Vermont

Edited by

Alice Wolf Gilborn, Rob Hunter
Carol Cone, Brenda Nicholson, Monica Stillman

D1527615

The Blueline Press
Danby, Vermont

Library of Congress Certificate of Registration Number:
TX 7-526-671

ISBN: 978-0-9620309-3-2

Cover paintings and interior artwork: Betsy B. Hubner
    Front cover: *Family Gathering*
    Back cover: *Before the Flight*

Layout: Alice Gilborn

Espresso Book Machine Coordinator: Debbi Wraga

Printed by The Shires Press
    Northshire Bookstore
    P.O. Box 2200
    Manchester Center, Vt. 05255
    northshire.com/printondemand

Published by The Blueline Press
    P.O. Box 175
    Danby, Vt. 05739
    thebluelinepressvermont.com

Credits for previously published work, pp. 112–113

Text is set in Garamond. Titles are in Book Antiqua.

Manufactured in the United States of America

Birchsong
Poetry Centered in Vermont

Contents

Preface

On the evening of August 27, 2011, five days before the deadline for submitting work to *Birchsong,* the first drops of rain of what became Tropical Storm Irene began to fall. Those of us living in Vermont know all too well what happened the next day. None of the poems in this volume were written after the devastation caused by the worst flooding since 1927—there was no time. As such, they have a certain prelapsarian quality, not always idyllic but before land and spirit suffered such a catastrophic upheaval.

Some of the poems, about previous floods and hurricanes, can be read prophetically. Others tell of ordinary life in a state without one large city: its landscape and seasons, its people and animals, the fulfillment of living close to the earth—and the hardship. Many speak of the weather, a neutral subject uniting native Vermonters and those who have chosen to come here for various reasons; not least among them, to find beauty and calm in the midst of a stormy world.

This book represents the work of many people, chiefly the poets but also the members of the poetry discussion group, the Northshire Poets, who became its editors. Though gratified when the mail yielded new submissions each day, we received many more poems than we were able to publish. We read them all, initially without knowing who wrote them. Finally, after several rounds of reading and many hours, we chose the work of fifty-six poets who live in Vermont or who are familiar with the region. Some of their poems have been previously published in other journals or books (see credits, p. 112); we are pleased to give them continued life in this anthology. Others are original to *Birchsong.* Whether reprinted or appearing here for the first time, narrative or lyrical, each poem, while centered in Vermont, travels well beyond its borders.

Alice Wolf Gilborn
Mount Tabor, Vermont

Acknowledgments

We wish to thank all those who submitted to *Birchsong,* whether we chose their work or not, for their effort, their patience, and for following directions. Thanks also to Burr and Burton Academy's Rob Hunter, our perceptive guest editor, and to Betsy Hubner who provided the excellent paintings on both covers and the interior artwork. We are indebted to the Northshire Bookstore for the use of its conference room for our deliberations, as well as to the bookstore's Debbi Wraga, wizard of the Espresso Book Machine, for her enthusiastic support of this project and her expert advice.

Birchsong

Pamela Ahlen

Ah, Spring,

sweet meadow pranked with green,
the red-winged blackbird
yessing a sweet potato sky.

But Mama Nature's playing
two-stick tricks, paradiddle
pandemonium all shake, rattle

and rain, all flash-frozen roof.
Sweet Mama's come undone,
her arctic farce unsheathed,

foolish snow bending forget-me-nots
and cuckoo flowers,
bowing birches to their knees.

Lawn Party

Let the grass
shake loose its green
and blaze orange
with fire of hawkweed.
Let the grass
grow purple heal-all,
pink forget-me-nots and
wild celandine. Let the grass
hear the violets
sing the blues, the yowls
of the white pussy-toes,
the snap-clap toe-tap
johnny jump-ups.
Let the grass
drink the golden wine
of dandelion,
raise a holy buttercup ruckus.

Wayside

Her grandfather dug the pond with one mule
and a stone sled. Winters she'd place the Victrola
on the ice, wind up Porter or Gershwin
and skate resilient. Come spring she'd harness Rosie
to the cart and trot the neighbor children up the road
past bloodroot and hepatica, past the pond
with its returning mallards and geese—
but not too early in spring, not like today,
Wayside a muddy ooze, patches of snow
still clinging to shady spots. A pair of geese
nest on the tiny island in the middle of the pond,
the island a new owner "from away" will submerge
because the geese offend him. Like the April snow,
country life's receding: farms, stories,
the rooted resiliency like old growth pines.
What's "oozing in" is tentacled, hormonal, engineered.
Sun warms our arms,
bare for the first time in months. We sit on her porch,
celebrate with cake and 98 candles, look out on the pond
imagining a Bruegel scene.

Ben Aleshire

Autumn Poem

Taking the road
  from the creek to the barn
you shuffle through rows
  of tumbled gold.
Even before reaching the stairs
  you can hear the insects
dying; you can hear the buzz
  of their slow death
in the attic. Ladybugs
  hide in your hair, cling
to your face for warmth as you see,
  through the gap in the burlap
curtains, the stallion:
  black and shimmering
muscles popping his
  nostrils flare his hot breath
streams out in violent puffs
  his snout like the barrel of a gun.
Restless, he charges one fence
  to the other. Again. Again.
How is it that his field of flowers
  has become a prison?

Hunting

We make a fleeting animal
—David Budbill

Down by the sleeping tracks
a pool of lake reflects the sky
pearl of moon   fortresses of cloud

We stand beholding it, clutching
at each other like love will slip away
with the spreading ripples we see

                                 this
is when the gunshot comes
from the mother beaver   her tail
slaps the surface, demanding us to leave.

She moves in the water   slow bullet
protecting her brood? And we ours—
We clutch tighter at the wild animal

caught between us   we try to tame it
this thing we've been hunting.

Stuart Bartow

Without Birds the Sky Would Not Exist

is what I tell the college class I am
visiting to discuss my book of poems
that has so many birds inside. They look
blankly back at me, not because they're foolish,
but shy. Despite what so many think, though
they're tattooed, flipflopped, and wear fake tans,
they are intelligent and kind. The world
has made them wary, passive, and they know
not to trust poets. Immediately I
prove to be a weirdo by turning out
the lights and raising the blinds. I talk
about sympathetic fallacy and
cosmic complicity but, of course,

the windows are sealed shut as I note we
too are caged. The skyline is empty
of birds this spring afternoon, yet I read
poems of flight. How I love the fact that nature
will not bend to our will. Or, perhaps it does,
always, but all that invisible force,
like dark matter, dark energy, constantly
competes, creates a kind of balance,
a gravity of wills which the sparrows,
who now I see careening
toward a far cupola, care nothing about.

Jeff Bernstein

Aeolus Comes to the Mountain

Most of the time that hike
ended in disappointment,
although the morning sky
was clear and dark oak beams
of the giant harp always glistened
in the sunlight. But once or twice,
it pivoted into the wind, fiddlehead
fern steel began to hum, calling
beyond Central Vermont
to other worlds. I am not sure

how my father first stumbled
upon it, but once he knew what was up
on that ridge he wanted to return
again and again to see the living vision
of one young Thomas McCain. Mornings,
McCain must have left his aerie, walked
fifty feet to the site. Two years
to build that hilltop concert hall,
birds, clouds and whatever Aeolus
would exhale his only diversions

except for that downhill trek
to Chelsea Post Office every few weeks
or so. Tom'd smile, politely answer
neighbors' questions as laconically
as they put them to him. "How's the harp
coming?" "Good." When his forty foot siren
was ready to sing the first time,
Tom's mom arrived from upstate New York
in a battered Ford, organized
a picnic for the villagers around the altar.

[more]

First bites of ham and cheese, pickled eggs
had no sooner touched their teeth
when the dampers were released
and the wind, given its liberty,
began to sing of its journey around
this watery sphere. Next morning, Tom loaded
a few possessions into raggedy pack-
frame, trudged down rocky trail until
he reached State Route 113, stuck out his thumb,
waiting to see where kind motorists might take him.

Slow Courting

"Thank you Ma'am," Uncle
would say on those one lane

ancient roads, cart tracks really,
when an ongoing vehicle

would pull off and let him
pass. Sometimes, it'd be

"if you please" instead,
when the dust was highest

and it wasn't clear which
car would give way

first. Bear in mind this happened
at about the pace of turtles

courting, males facing females,
slowly nodding their heads up

and down, side to side
hours at a time.

Partridge Boswell

Forty Words

I did not go into the meadow
did not steal through that
wide open window to lay
in tall grass or short grass
how can I say which grass
I did not get into that grass
at all

nor watch the milkweed rise
from our porch it wasn't anything
I could see beyond stonewall/
row of trees never stepped
through the gap there or
stood in the dying sun & took
my leave

it wasn't anything from where
I stood no sleight-hand of heaven
here on earth no slice of strawberry
rhubarb blueberry peach or any
other said with a sigh the wild
carrot knows too well the brush
of thigh

it never felt like summer at all
though we watched trees leaf
and melt into each other's green
grace don't let me tell you there
wasn't love there & plenty
not more than forty words from
this place

Just Remember I Knew You When

Prime example I'm apt to cite is Lenny,
who forked his mind's manure for years
caretaking that north-sloping, hill-hunched
farm while chasing down a MFA as if it were

a cagey ewe, so he could justify the hours
between feedings and mending fences.
Shelved screenplays stacked like hay bales
in disheveled abandon beside an enormous

cookie jar of pennies, one saved for every
stagnant phrase exhumed and dragged
from the tomb of process. Every dispensation
of hay leaf and grain, he'd dream of stuffing

that wadding into his hometown's canon,
waiting for the fuse to catch, the flint to knock
smartly against the frizzen making sparks,
the charge to leap into the barrel, followed

at length by distant bursting. Who could say
how far its arc might reach, what town
might wake and think fireworks or lightning?
And when lo at last the powder did ignite

you could see it in his eyes. A Hollywood
contract, front page of the local weekly,
daily calls from an agent whose sun-drenched
assurances and mineral water excuses blurred

whatever artificial differential once existed
between coasts. Could he hear his own
lightly dredged laughter at parties, cynical
lemon twist of luck he wished a recent graduate

brave enough to admit she was trying her uncalloused
hand at short fiction? Could he taste the gelignite
of early fame rising in the back of his throat,
his saliva now an appraised thing?

The month on the lot, holding more strings
than a director, actors turning in their mouths
the fruit from his own backyard trees,
asking permission to pick & eat. Rumors inflate

like Macy's balloons till we figure, well, that's
the last this shrunken pond will see of him . . .
but then he's filling up at the Teago pump,
looking the same old sheenless penny

as if he'd never left, no guy ropes dangling
like dreadlocks from his head. So, I ask,
when are we going to see that world premiere
at the Town Hall? Oh that, he sneers,

I wouldn't let my own daughter watch that shit
and climbs in his truck. We wait a year or so
and finally forget before unearthing it
in the action-adventure racks of a big city

video store. A sci-fi western about prospecting
for gold on another planet, maybe you've seen it:
the marvelously abundant myriad of expletives
available to every life form, the sample of each

character's persona maculate to the core.
We endured for twenty hard fought minutes
before giving up. You know it's bad when your
fiancée says nudity would have improved it.

His daughter's in high school now. He manages
his father's lumberyard where at least there's
an identifiable smell, the whine of saws
biting into something that once grew.

Regina Murray Brault

Mother Tongue

In the trailer park
where diapers snap on clotheslines
like flags in semaphore
the child cradled in my arms
lies swaddled in
the rhythms of her world.

She hears a thrush song
from the thicket
and searches with her eyes.
bird I tell her
and wish her wings.

And when she shivers to the breeze
that shakes brown needles
from their boughs
I whisper *wind*
and wish her grace.

She looks to me
while sprinkles dance staccato
on our metal roof.
rain I say
and wish her gentleness.

She gathers all these sounds of life
like nosegays edged in baby's breath
and stores them in her throat.
Then, in a voice
as soft as summer showers
meadow music
whiffs of wind

she names me *Mama.*

T. Alan Broughton

Late Raking

My aging neighbor tries to pick up
the rake that slipped from his grasp.
He stands, hand on his ailing hip,
and stares at the stubborn handle
as my father would when he blamed
his fingers' width for dropping screws.
His lips move, but he's too polite
to say aloud what he thinks.

He succeeds on the next try,
begins again to scrape last leaves
into a pile the north wind scatters
before he can bag them. I should
leave my window, cross the lawn
bearing a rake, divert his need
to warn me off by rousing
his anger as I report the latest
city tax. I lean one hand against
the glass, palm spread as if it is
a bird flown into stunning clarity,
heart fluttering once as I recall
how often as my father bent
beneath the years I could not bear
to witness, I watched, trapped
in tangles of pity and fear
for what I could not accept.

[more]

When he lost words as we talked,
he must have seen my eyes become
porcelain, the spirit behind them
retreating—to where? Was it love
that would not admit an image
of his coming death, denial
so deep and cold that even now,
watching my neighbor try to keep
a bag from filling like a sail,
the place where my heart should be
is only a cavity, a cave of loss
I cannot fill even though I invade,
brandishing a rake, calling his name.

Closure

In a hesitant fall even trees are indecisive,
a motley of green and gold or tarnished brown
disheveled by northern eddies of air
that sullenly retreat before persisting sun;
and streams, denied their steady season
of rain, shrink, exposing worn stone
and trout writhing like trapped eels.

No matter, I must close the house again.
Coy warmth won't last for long, and frost
will rime the roof I've swept. Soon comes
heft of first wet snow. Fill closets, cover beds
with plastic sheets, and nail all windows
shut that have lost their clasps. Mice
will move in briefly, feeding on d-con.

Where will winter take me?
From my perch on a sunny rock,
back against shingles of this house
where I've loved and waked again
and again from un-deciphered dreams,
I see cairns in the glade marking
the ground where my parents' ashes lie.

Duties are done, each room battened down.
Ravens croak on distant cliffs,
red squirrels scold *go, go home.*
Leave this place to listless bumbling
of last bees while leaves are pressed
into the sleep of certainty beyond cold,
and joists settle under dead weight.

Joseph Bruchac

Returning Geese

Wearing the long feathers of snow,

wearing the black masks of night,

speaking the language of clouds,

they cross the sky

above Lake Bomoseen.

Can we understand

the call that brings them

over these small places

where we live?

Can we, too,

have such courage

to trust the wild,

to know many lands,

to return to homes

so changed by strangers' hands?

By Way of Apology

The tiny insect that appears on your finger
after you pick up a pine branch
is smaller than an afterthought,
more fragile than a spider's strand,
as easily brushed into oblivion
as that relationship between you
and the person for whom you care
despite the hurtful words you spoke.

So, take another careful breath
and, as if whispering syllables of regret,
lean close to the August blooming
red geraniums in the gray stone planter
then breathe, fluttering its minuscule
lace wings until it is wafted off
to land safely in the green leaves there
like a blessing, a forgiveness,
a life you both still share.

Judith Chalmer

navigator

strict lines
dark winter road
your ivory sweater

and once your hand
left the wheel
just as I was trying
not to regret-

regret, a kind
of amulet—

your hand on mine
your voice that one
of popcorn and rum
sunny afternoons
at home, a pile of books
going nowhere hard

and still I fear
love, I could never
get there without you

Anna Chapman

Moving Day on Route 7

There goes a U-Haul
over cracks in the road
made by last winter's frost
past the place where a deer
was demolished at night
leaving only a brownish-red
smear on the tarmac
and wisps of coarse hair
stuck to dry cornstalks
next to a derelict
barn whose west gable
is shedding its shingles
which though they drop slowly
fall faster than the man
at the wheel of the U-Haul
can hope to remove
the marks of his life
from the place he's just left
though he's sure he has gone

Elayne Clift

Signs of Vermont

Here, between *frost heaves* and a *narrow bridge*,
Amid church reminders that ask—
If God seems absent, guess who moved?—
Among *Flea Markets* and *Pick Your Own* pumpkins,
Here, where *Sabra Field* and *Simon Pearce* reign,
Perhaps there are *Fresh Eggs*, or *Quilts*, or *Syrup Ahead!*
In this land of *moose* and deer, and
Spirit of Health holistic healing,
where a *Coop* offers only *all natural* foods,
and where *Main Street* meets *Mountain Road*,
Where *Ben and Jerry's*, or *Green Mountain Coffee*
and *Cabot cheese* are on offer at the *Country Store*,
Where *Pottery* and *Antiques* mix with *Welding*
and *Wood for Sale*, here
May Peace Prevail on Earth, and may we all
Experience Deceleration.

Carol Cone

When We Sold The Canoe

When we sold the canoe that fall
We threw in thirty memorable years

We launched her in every lake in Vermont
Bomoseen, Willoughby, Victory Bog

Gale Meadows Pond and the reservoir
Rising out of the predawn mist

Tracking steelhead and northern pike
Brown trout, rainbow and smallmouth bass

Silent but for the sound of oars, or
Sometimes the call of an osprey or loon

Watching the heron leave its nest,
The wake of a beaver swimming away

When we sold the canoe that fall
We threw in maps and fishing guides

The rod and reel, the electric motor
The battery, cushions and tackle box

Just forty pounds of light aluminum
Painted to look like real birchbark

"Light as a feather," the catalog said,
"Pop it on top of the car and go!"

But forty pounds of aluminum
Doubles its weight as the years go by

That's why we sold the canoe that fall
But sometimes in my dreams I still

Feel something tugging on my line
A bass, a trout, a prize winning catch

In dreams we still can lift the boat.

Greg Delanty

Driving in Vermont

The trees descend from the mountains in plumes of leaf-fire
        that people travel thousands of miles
to admire, but how many spot the god taking a break
        from Delphi? Nobody asks him to dish out prophesy today.
Perhaps they're too afraid to know what lies ahead.
        I bet he came on the urging of an Abenaki deity
in the egalitarian realm of the gods.
        Folk drive by, their radios reporting
the weather, last night's frost, baseball, the demise of the world
        in the umpteen ways we've devised, maybe a few comment
on the glorious light, everyone hightailing it to work. But now
        my job is to pull off Route 15 at Hyde Park and Centerville
and report this sighting. Who'd have thought the god
        of light would be seen in the North East Kingdom,
Apollo himself, on the lam from his Attic stomping ground.

Arlene Distler

The Case Against Mums

I refuse to plant mums
or set them apron-prim
in pots along my walk.
What have they to say
that hasn't been said before?

I prefer autumn's tawdry mix
of unkempt rows,
sunflower's swollen prose,
stripped-down lily's
arcs of green
turned shadowy wisps,

maple leaves' last fling
with sun,
doomed to fatal swoon
when day's undone.

I'd rather not extend
the reign of floral domain
with stingy pots of color spots
when wild fall is all about—
the straggly romance
of late blooming petunia

twined in Glory blue,
promiscuous phlox
in all its hues,
milkweed's blousy tufts
drifted who knows where.

The day bud's last flower
is all I need of the hour.

Danny Dover

Gathering
—for Steve Killam

In the beginning
was glacial rock
gathered into stony soil
which gathered these maples
which now gather us
gathering fresh sap
as March air softens
slabs of deep snow,
stumbling on snowshoes
toward the steamy arch
with buckets brimming
buzzing like honeybees
around a sweet boiling brew,
waking from winter's isolation
with home-made wine
and ginger snaps
fleece jackets unzipped
by a blazing firebox
gathering the hours,
gathering news and tales
of friends in need,
gathering time
in boiled-down years
toward a moment
of distillation
that gathers the best
we can bring to each other,
liquid treasure poured
thick and sweet,
a glowing amber
cherished in the brilliant
April morning light

A bat is living

The faint soft rustle
flutters like dragonflies
in a dark cramped cavity
of the bow
A bat

is living in my canoe

Probably nested under the shed roof
since March, then three rough hours
on a car rack to this first paddle
of spring

Only the two of us out here
on stillwater rousing from winter,
drumming wingbeats against
a mist-and-cedar-rimmed shore
flaming in sunrise

Tractor Man

Fifteen summers I've passed you
on the same stretch of dirt road
back behind the Third Branch
of the White River, a bedraggled
lump of wild beard and splayed
knees stuffed onto your tiny
worn-out lawn tractor stuck in
first gear, sputter-crawling four
miles from town to a hardscrabble
farmhouse with empty barn and
hayfields long gone to seed.
I go there to run, to coax
another season's cycle from
an aging body slowed down
a notch each year, loping
by without a word, my hand
tossed out in a humble wave
hardly masking a smug sense
of agility and superior fitness.
So we pass,

and time passes both the hare
and the tortoise, slumped further
into your John Deere shell, beard
grown shaggier though in my heart
I know we shall cross the same finish
line, you and I, someday with our
perfect bodies and breathless faces
glowing pink with purpose
and pride, a job well done.

George Drew

Instructions for Sitting on the Famous
Poet's Porch

Forget the mountains and all things distant.
Begin by examining the phlox and other plants
that have over the years grown ever taller,
and through the opening between the trees
across the road the birds that drift by slowly,
winging westward, toward Vermont.
You should be alone, preferably at dusk,
and pondering the roots of Latinate words,
for instance *Tulis*, and if they mean something
significant or are nothing more than mundane.
Then think about *all* the famous poets
who have trod the porch from one end
to the other, all the poets who have sat on it,
the poets who have drunk and eaten there,
and have made love to it through their poems.
Think about all the feet that have trod on it,
and then about the feet that eventually will
never tread again its old gray peeling boards.
Be grateful, and then for God's sake sit
yourself down and write a poem of your own.
We will read it and praise you for it,
and in your honor we will drink wine
as red and fullbodied as that which Horace
drank to honor his friend and benefactor, Maecenas.
When the sun has disappeared behind the mountains
and you are ready depart, but when you do
step lightly, avoid the boards that creak,
and leave everything exactly as you found it.
The eyes you can feel watching your every move
most likely are the squirrels'. But you never know.

Elegy for Jared

Once there was a mountain named Panther,
and on this mountain lived a family.
There was a father, a mother, and a son.
In the story old Vermonters like to tell
no one knows what kind of tree it was the father cut,
and he was so hobbled by a father's horror
he never could recall. Some like to think it was a birch,
its bark as white and tight as the soul
of such a little boy—four years old, maybe five.
But that's too fairy tale. More likely it was oak or maple.
What *is* known is that the boy had come
to call his father in to dinner
and that at the exact moment the father heard
his son's sprightly voice riding the breeze
the tree commenced its downward rush,
right toward the boy. It killed him instantly.

Now, him. Sometimes we were friends,
sometimes less, sometimes more.
Surely we shared a love of bad habits,
even if for him they were a calling—
heart giving out like that and him only fifty
and the one I always thought the stronger.
Unlike the father of the boy,
who must have borne the weight of that tree
throughout his hardscrabble life,
I won't water his plot with half-willed tears.
For on the great talus slope of time
our lives bisected only for the heartbeat
that it took the second-growth forest
to fall before the axes of the settlers
and the smelters' need for tons and tons
of charcoal to fashion in their furnaces
the real bedrock of the Republic—iron.
Now the forest has come back in Vermont,
and in the forest the panther—him of the green eyes
and muscles rippling under swarthy skin,
his scat smoking as he slips through the forest
more shadow than cat, forever unseen but there.
The mountain once called Panther is Panther again.

The Birch in which the Grouse was Sitting

Really, I'm not asking a lot—some water,
ice please, a salad with poppyseed dressing,
the same as last time. It was luscious!
For the main course cod cakes, and on the side
baked beans and summer squash. No dessert,
just coffee. Can you handle that? I know,
you're scattered, had a horrible day. Your feet hurt,
you're on alone again, with too many tables,
and naturally the whole damned village is here,
and it only Thursday. Well, it's not my doing,
I'm just passing through, and I tip big—
fifteen percent, twenty if you keep my coffee hot.
Forget the other customers! I was here first,
and I've already waited forty minutes. Look,
I'm not asking for oceans, only ponds,
even one clogged with algae and lilypads—
if you get the metaphor. You don't?
Basically, I want to be hard for you to get
rid of. I want to be the ruffed grouse
I saw today along a trail. It was in a tree
and I stood for a long time eyeing it,
waiting it out. After awhile I moved my hand,
an arm, but it wouldn't take flight,
just eyed me back, puffed its throat.
I was determined, but not as much as it.
It stayed, never even spreading its feathers,
and I gave in. Leaving it there on its limb,
I moved on…. No, no, I don't want *you* to go
away, at least no farther than the kitchen.
What *do* I want? I want to be for you
like the birch in which the grouse was sitting—
so dazzling I blind you into liking me.
Now run along—and don't forget the bread:
no butter, and tartar sauce. I'll get the water.

Linda Durkee

To Begin Again

The answer came before the question.
In one stroke of good luck
I found a place to live
in the meadow of my middle years,
a once-upon-a-time barn
in the valley of Mount Tabor.
Cows slept in the basement,
horses graced the kitchen,
hay piled up in the loft, all long gone now
but for echoes of girls and boys playing tag,
three- and four-leaf clover stippling the sloping lawn,
the small shed stilled, its red door locked.
I make hay while the sun shines. There's more.
I count locust trees among my blessings,
Apples too, tufted tit mice, and black-capped chickadees.
I have the urge to dream.
My grandfather had a farm, his father too.
Here, past and future merge.
I was told a spiral staircase needs a room
with a curved wall. There is one, skylight too.
Sun stokes the kitchen with a southerly view.
Wide pine planks stride the floor.
On every side, windows catch the hue
and brew of seasons changing.
To my city-shuttered eyes, I marvel
as stars bejewel the sky.
A full moon beamed this fall
through the octagon window in my bedroom wall.
Mornings, flatbed trucks roll by,
hauling to fabled marble halls
precision-cut imperial white.
Pearl mists drape the hills,
remnants of the chilly night.
Rarely in December, often in July,
Shoosh, my elegant neighbor cat, drops by.
This year, the snow came late.
I live thus in my house,
in the cradle of my new beginning,
as warm and cool
as slate.

Florence Fogelin

Scapes

I'm back again from places picture-perfect,
Tuscany this time, a sunlit dream
where every hill town punctuates its presence—
trim rows of cypress trees, elegant and precise.
Back to Partridge Lake,
the spring-fed, snow-filled, muddy wet of it.

From Italian gardens and city boulevards
defined and caged by geometry—
hedges, topiary, pear trees splayed against a wall,
walks swept impossibly clean, even dirt and gravel.
Back to where the soil's so poor
it needs a granite bed to hold the lake in place.
Again the rebellious mix of pine, birch, and hardwoods
quarreling for a patch of light,
strangling rocks in search of food so scarce
ancestral rot is nourishment.
In this familiar clearing in the woods,
the undergrowth welcomes strangeness
in a mushroom, the careless ease of ferns.

Lené Gary

from the edge of the reservoir

at first there is no water, there is no land
there is only

      white

you can somehow stick your fingers through
& wiggle, maybe see the tips before they numb
in the cold of an early morning fog

a part of you wants to see what lies beyond
the weightless veil you cannot move
another part decides

you like living in a cloud

then (as always) a mountain range you've forgotten
will inhale, deeply pulling that curtain before your eyes

rusty goldenrods, tufts of grass

a few lemon-colored leaves on smoky branches
a breeze you cannot feel, water blue

the color of the sky, as clear as ever in your life
only a whisper of that early white remains, sliding
towards the narrow place

where you must paddle
left or right

Bishop's Weed

Her favorite garden is not a garden at all but a large patch (or small pocket) of bishop's weed behind the barn. Sometimes there is madder wafting honey in the air, but by far, this plot of uncultivated land is dominated by one plant tall enough to be considered *erotically invasive*. So thick as to create a nesting place for love, so tall as to create a picket fence of flowering proportion, so tender as to cushion the barest back of man, it becomes her preferred bedstraw in the deep Sunday of July when he stands over her with a sheet in hand.

Kirk Glaser

Element of May

Where water births in the hills,
steam shudders through trees and breaks into run.
In the last hour of light, I hunt trillium to put by your bed.
Under the dank growth of ferns, their white
and scarlet eyes bend to the ground and smolder.

Strange sensation: I think an angel crouches in a tree
to watch the burn of flowers and mist.
Fidgeting, he sets a branch to shake
and knocks fat drops off apple blossoms.
The little cat, leaping at a moth,
darts from the barrage of tree-rain
while the big one lazes, grown accustomed
to the reel of summers.

What is it in this momentary light—
the disc of sun broken through rain clouds
low on the hills—that transfuses the field,
tree frog clamor and the soughing blow of a horse
with a liquid clear and dense as quartz?

If we could become the element we mostly are,
pour into the ground and air, we could cross
like a wing of steam over this leadened etching of land,
or prod our way to a flowering head.
But love comes to us, acid-bathes us,
when all we think we want is to fill
the warm hollows of our bellies and legs,
to spend our lives heavy, fleshed out of earth.

Flood Storm

—On the banks of the Ompompanoosuc River, Thetford, Vermont

Where did the butterfly
spend the fierce night?
Hanging over flooded earth
from milkweed stem without a thought
tucked beneath the leaf's pale underside,
wings pressed shut against rain and wind
still save for the swell and collapse
of the body breathing at their base
for which the wings exist.
Or does the body exist for them?

On the bank in a pile of clothes
insects make home,
the crease in the paper
tucked in a pocket
a good dark place to hide
and release a silver burden of eggs.

Spiders sun on the beached plank raft,
gray sacks bigger than themselves
hooked to their abdomens
risking bird's eye
for the dry, hot, fertilizing light
to hatch their brood.
They trust to lightning legs—
little to do but act as if
we all will reach fruition,
not plucked up in another's mouth.

Let worry go
says the spider flinging
filaments from blade to blade
of grass over the bank
where yesterday's rain-flood
swept away the world.

Barry Goldensohn

Saint Jerome's Vale

"...withdraw to patience and meekness
for we must first descend in order to be raised."

One, watching from a train or driving
oxcart curves in a sleek car, veering
past a pine that towers above the spire
of the bare church considers the scale too small,
a cell called "little ease"—an instrument
in which one can not stand or lie or sit—
or slow suffocation in a tight box—
a gas station yoked to a general store,
a post office and not much more around
a modest square with its modest monument
to its Civil War dead with the following wars
inscribed below. It seems to the traveler
he could cover the town with his hand.
And yet from behind the pillars on the porch
or the neat front yards, enclosed by the walls
of house and shed and barn, and other yards,
a homegrown labyrinth in which a world
of delight and lust, women and men, faces
and bodies, eyes that know you deeply—

she has stumbled downstairs, wrapped
in a quilt she made, drawn by the smell
of fresh brewed coffee, a beautiful woman
of middle age, barely awake, waves
of bed-warmth radiate from the naked self
engulfed in its gown of goose down and cotton,
and waits by the window for the day to fill in.
All the obstacles that passion overcomes
are here full size. From a large world
a car climbs the hill and looks down on a village
in which a woman any man would love
waits to greet a day that offers her little things:
coffee, a man, a job, a child, a book.

Vermont Walks

1

From Churchill Road, along the Bothfeld farm,
low clouds are incandescent in the valleys
and light the hills from below—a distant beauty,
not human. What sits up close
is well used land. Stubble in parallel lines
that undulate along the curve of cornfields—the lengths
of cut stalks of stubble in right proportion
to the distance between the rows. Every thing
in perfect rhythm with the shape of the land
as we move past in a flurry of bright leaves
from the file of sugar maples and the fresh stink
of manure blowing through the shining valleys around us.

2

Even the road is abandoned. The forest around us
nearly a century old. Stone walls
that divided meadow and pasture, field
and road, now slice through unbroken woodland.
Surrounded by dead lilacs, cellar holes
fill with dead mufflers, tailpipes, tires.
We stamp our way through weeds that fill the ruts
that mark a wagon road too steep for horses.
These lost fields were farmed with oxen, now
it won't pay to clear these woods again.
They thicken and welcome home cougar and wolf,
the Abenaki have vanished beyond recall.

3

Well past noon, the world at gainful work,
young, we walked with poem talk and hunger
across a field of sweet summer grass,
our path the breastbone of a giant nude
with rounded hills sighing on either side
in the breeze through the waves of the tall grass.
At the deepest point in the bright breathing valley
we stopped and seized the purpose of our walk
and tumbled to making love as the sun stood by
for our familiar wild caresses, quicksilver limbs
covered with faint sweat. The earth seemed ours,
sufficient to our pleasure in one another.

Jack Gundy

Spring Harvest

Down a narrow corridor

cut through five-foot snow banks

the sugarhouse roars

with steel pans of bubbling

sap collected from

a thousand maples.

Searing flames leap out

open boiler doors

as Susi pushes in

four-foot birch slabs,

then reads the hydrometer,

calls out specific

gravities to her husband,

Jack, who opens a brass

valve to the filter press.

Their voices marry

with the thin blood of trees

boiling down

to sweet liquid amber.

Kathleen McKinley Harris

Work Ethic

It's different, our father explained.
This summer you must pay for candy
and soda pop you take from behind the counter.
Your great aunt and uncle have been too good. They've
allowed too many in town to run up big tabs,
and they're too kind to ask poor people to pay up.

That summer Great Uncle kept half a dozen
    young Jerseys
in his mother's small barn down the road where
there was no pasture, so he cut fresh green hay with a scythe
    as feed,
milked morning and night before he opened the store.
Next summer Great Aunt and Uncle's general store
    and garage
with red flying horse sign and a complete house upstairs
—back verandah, kitchen, dining room, living room, long
    hall, bedrooms—
had new owners. And Great Aunt and Uncle owned a large,
    rundown farm
across the valley on Battle Row. Great Uncle, his sons,
    and hired men
replaced every ruined fence on the place with sound,
    stout cedar posts
and three taut wires, cleared fencerows, first time
    in fifty years.
Even I, a child, could see the pastures and fields come back,
hear pride in Great Uncle's voice at what he'd done with
    vision, hard work, and will—
a new beginning when he and Great Aunt were not young,
he whose recreation was going to Hicks' weekly cattle
    auction—
success depending not solely on the land but also on his
    being a fine judge of cows—
or driving on the Bayley-Hazen Road on a cool evening.
My father worried Great Aunt didn't have enough fun
    in her life.

[more]

Great Uncle couldn't understand how my father could let
his land grow up into weed trees, blackberries, ferns—
not keep the fields and pastures clean.
Great Uncle's standards inside his barn were as high
as outside. Children were not allowed to jump
in his hay mow and damage the cows' feed.
His gutters were cleaned immediately, strewn with bedding.
He received a premium for his milk's low bacterial count.
My father pointed out Great Aunt's cleanliness
    in the milk house
contributed to their achievement, gave credit where
    it was due.
We'd talk about horses, Great Uncle and I.
I'd tell him about my mare. He told me how he hated
to trade his horses for a dirty, smelly, noisy tractor.
Then the times forced him to give up his beautiful Jerseys
for black and white Holsteins, put in a bulk tank, too.
Daily Great Aunt fried doughnuts for his breakfast.
He lived on fresh doughnuts, pie, coffee, cigarettes,
meat and potatoes, doomed himself to stomach cancer—
finally died of it. He milked the day he died.

David Huddle

Drinking Alone by Moonlight
—*after Li Bai's "Drinking Alone By Moonlight"*

The moon damns a man drinking wine alone—
he'd wanted to bloom in the silver light
but the intimacy he found was with himself,
the cup he lifted purest solitude. So many

people hovering in the shadows—he couldn't
understand the sounds he heard. *My body
is out here, too!* he shouted. Into the silence
that followed he whispered, *Is this temporary?*

Wine cheers a fellow, he thought. It'll be
spring soon. Ah, but the damning moon shone
ruthlessly across his arms and shoulders.
The man shuffled his feet, told them to dance,

but no one emerged from the shadows to become
his friend. The man imagined himself as cinders
scattered over dirt and pavement, ashes sifted into
water. Then the man understood the moon was about

to disperse him out into the great river of stars.
He'd have to sober up, have to stop whining. But oh,
the place he was going would be his companion—he'd be
the cloud, she the sunlight blazing him up gold.

Finch Dream

Baby-fist-sized darts of gold streak the air
around feeder and bath, they weave in low
around porch posts, swerve past house, tree, and car.

Local angels, these spring-crazed finches are
hot for each other, sun-drops of yellow
we miss if we blink, gold looping the air.

Rocketing our planet toward hell, we're
disconsolate, staring out our windows
at blurred birds zipping past house, tree, and car—

their flighty exuberance stops us where
we stand. Small brains, tiny hearts, do they know
how we oafs feel when their gold fires the air?

Once I walked through high grass where hundreds were
feeding and they flew up before me, they rose
like a dream—no houses or cars, just birds

rising in swooping arcs, splotches of fire
invented by the sky and the spring meadow.
I walked among gold flashes streaking the air.
Houses and cars all gone. Finches everywhere.

From Deep Down in My Work, I Hear a Call

Flying toward my house this morning the geese
make a racket that makes me almost without thought
set my laptop aside, stand up, and step quickly

out onto my porch—then out onto the grass. They
make me raise my face toward their clamor: low
overhead, wings whistling, their bellies golden

in October light, thirty or so that sound
like hundreds generating a sociable ruckus
in complaint or praise of the great seasonal

upheaval dispatching them wherever they're headed.
Then—and this is the luck a day will sometimes
grant me, a wish I haven't sense enough to realize,

a random perfection—in utter silence a turkey vulture
sails across even lower than the geese and at an angle
near enough I see how its flight feathers shift. This

is not about the chill that shivers me
when the geese and the majestic scavenger
have passed, not about my desire to return

to my work and my computer, the warmth
of my house or my soft sofa. It's about
that half an instant of standing alone

under a sky the nameless blue of my infant dreams,
among the trees gone yellow and orange, the still
air clear as a soprano's hitting and holding E

above high C with the day just begun and the whole
raw world summoning me to step through a door
I can't even see.

Rob Hunter

September Swim

Knee deep just feet from shore
your dive was more of an unhurried fall,

your hands ahead of you,
and then the water closed around your clothes,

your skirt collapsing suddenly
like a flower pulled by its stem through liquid.

You didn't make a sound.
The wind rustled leaves all around us

and corrugated the water.
The sun dipped lower.

I didn't know if you would ever
appear again because in that split second,

standing on the shore of this pond
in the mountains, long afternoon shadows

were black shrouds on the water,
tinges of yellow and orange already

seeping into leaves, I sensed the new season,
felt one season expire and pass on.

And in that moment you were submerged,
swallowed whole; but like a loon,

you bobbed up and shrieked the cold
baptism out of your lungs. You then stood up,

wet clothes clinging to your body,
your hands holding your surprised face.

Greg Joly

Town Meeting

Alright—
we have a motion on the floor
to increase the town's
contribution to the county
animal shelter by $100.
Do I have a second?
Thank you, Frannie.
The motion has been seconded.
Now, is there any discussion
to come before this body?
Yes, Walter...

We needed a cat.
So we called that shelter.
Needed one to keep
the mice down on the farm.
They sent us a stack a' forms
and wanted at least three
character references.
Then they told us the farm
was too dangerous for a cat.
So we said fine
we'll keep the cat up to the house.
Nope. They said the house
is too close to the road.
All we wanted
was a god-damn
cat nobody else wanted.
Seems to me,
those people down
there rather kill a good cat
than give it a good home.

Walter,
I take it that
you are speaking
against the motion?

By Jesus—
That's how I'd read it.

Phyllis Beck Katz

Union Village Dam, Spring Flood 2011

I walk towards the silence that calls me
from the noises of this world: blaring music,
sirens, beeps of horns, voices using words
or telling stories I do not want to hear.
I climb up past the last house beyond the turning
where the roiling water born of this year's great spring rains,
tumbles through the tunnel and flows roaring out
beneath the dam swelling the river banks as it goes.
I stand on the giant edifice of stones and concrete
built so many years ago to hold back the floods
that once devoured the towns below its massive slope
and see a spreading lake where before the waters
rose so high, there were near-dry rivulets
meandering slowly through stagnant mud,
matted cat-tails, clotted clumps of honey-suckle,
and sand banks tracked by sandpipers and sparrows,
but where now still water widens over trees and trails,
haven for rafts of ducks resting from long flights,
for silhouettes of hawks and ravens gliding
across the clear surface, for logs floating free.
I look down into the water's depths and see
another world there untouched by life's loud intrusions,
and though the lake will slowly sink, the dirt roads
and trails, song birds nesting in the brush, return,
I do not want this earth to dry again. I want
to hold this silence born of water, to dive
into this deeper world—and stay.

Pumpkins on the River

When the clouds burst
and torrents of rain fell down
after days and days of drought,
the dry earth opened wide
its parched lips to drink,
and the river filled with
gladness, swelling above
its thirsty banks and
flooding a wide field
full of ripened pumpkins.
One by one the pumpkins,
wrested from their stalks
by the rising water,
floated away
from their roots
and left the soil
where they had grown.
You could see lines
of liberated pumpkins
stretching for miles,
moving to the river's
pull. For them, no rude
cutting of their flesh
into faces they did not
know, no wrenching out
of guts and seeds,
no candle scorching
their hollowed bellies,
no boiling, baking, stewing,
roasting. Free, they sailed
on unharmed, nodding gently
to the moving current,
as if consenting to its will,
and as they passed,
I longed to join them,
to follow as they journeyed
down-river to the sea.

Jean L. Kreiling

Wishing for Snow

If only winter's knife-edged cold would bend
and break and finally disintegrate
in tiny crystal fragments, we'd defend
our driveways and our walks, and celebrate
our strength. If only this unyielding sky
would soften and dissolve into a mist
of icy flakes, we'd raise an awestruck eye
to watch their fall. But winter likes to twist
the knife, to maximize its penetration
and coolly signal its supremacy,
withholding postcard-pretty compensation
for its cold shoulder, broad but bitterly
unbending. Empty, numbing air says "no":
no winter wonderland this time—no snow.

To a Hummingbird

Oh, blur of bird!

Please teach me how to hover weightlessly,
exquisitely escaping gravity,
and how to reach the speed of shimmering
and shapelessness, so that my movements sing.

Please show me how to flutter in reverse—
disturbing destiny, foiling a curse—
and how to find in bugs the nourishment
that nectar lacks. Teach me to be content

with pleasures blurred.

Lyn Lifshin

Cove Point

Some afternoons, in a certain
mood, there's a word, a name
I have to remember. Some
times it's for no reason: the
twins I never could remember
till I thought of cameras in the
attic: Garret and Cameron.
Yesterday it was the ramshackle
casino, its name over the lake
where, for the first time, in
white shorts and tan legs, my
heart banged: would I be
asked to dance? And what of
"The Mocking Bird" with its
kiss her in the center if you
dare. You have to remember,
I was the plump girl with
glasses of course I didn't wear
those nights so a lot blurred.
I was the girl who won science
contests and art awards. To have
boys who didn't know I was
brainy, ask will I… was like
heroin. "Ramshackle Pavilion"
in a lost student's poem sent me
to Google, to Lake Dunmore,
Branbury Beach: nothing. I knew
it burned down as if it never had
been there. Chimney Point? No.
With so many of my friends
going, the name of this dance hall
where I first felt pretty is a comfort
I'm starved for. I email Vt. tourist
sites, history sites with little
hope until in a warm tub I think:

[more]

diary, the little red one with a
lock that never worked there
near the bed. I turn to August
and there it was with seven
exclamation points and what I'd
been hunting for in so many
ways: Cove Point.

Daniel Lusk

Bull on the Roof

These frogs saved the world.
These frogs, fornicating in the lonely pond,
and these others singing all night in the trees.
They saved the world for silence.

All summer the rock cliff rises
behind the woods in secret,
looming behind birches and oak saplings,
their murmuring shadows suggesting voices
of soft-furred women in trees,
their elegant tails draping the branches.

These are images from a dream
I want not to wake from,
a dream where all the women's breasts freshen,
and I am the only child.

High overhead, bursts of east light
between stiff trunks thrust up
from roots anchored in rock, penetrating
the hidden places. As if winter
lived in a small house there,
next door to wind that blows only at night.

Among these wet caves there is nothing
I am afraid of. Not the yellow-spotted
salamander in the mud. Not the mud.
Not the libidinous jack-in-the-pulpit.

I fold my clothes, unfold my body
on a sundrenched rock
and listen to the hairy woodpecker at work.

[more]

One day when earth is exhausted
with pushing up and weary of swallowing.
When grouse tire of drumming.
When the brown-headed cowbird
has flown off with his bell
and the nests are empty.
When you and I
are like animals of the forest,
sated with heat.
When leaves give way to the rain
and weight of the sky.

We will go indoors to wait for the snow.
Winter will descend from its house.
The cliff will move closer
with icy teeth, huge in its power.

We will turn our backs and sit close to the fire.
We will hear the bull on the roof.
We will dream bright meadows and running water.

Uncle Charlie & Mole

My great-uncle Charles was blind.
Sat next to Grandma's spinet-legged radio:
thin music, tinny war correspondent voices
turned up loud. Faced the window south,
rocking chair back to the coal stove
where I sat on the bustle stool to daydream
when I was bored with my book.

The story the cock grouse told
to the hen grouse was about the giant
and the king's three best teeth
and the cake, the crutch and the cure.

Today my story has a dead mole.

I don't know how he came to be
on winter's tired battlefield.

That's how it looked—the matted
grass, leaf litter, maze of trenches
where small digging beasts waged war
on cold and hunger in our yard,
out of sight beneath the snow.

I admired how Uncle Charlie worked
those butterflies of leather from the bag
beside his chair into piecework belts
with his stubby hands. How his spatulated fingers
plied the wooden crochet hook, deftly
knotting shreds of dresses into oval rugs.

These aimless tunnels in our yard
show no such purpose.
Mole dug his way, bare-flippered,
like a little walrus, delicate pink hind feet

[more]

kicked out a wake of severed grassroots,
worm feces, moss breath.
Swam efficiently in dirt.

I compare the mole to Uncle Charles,
whose prayers were smoke rings
I believe he never saw. A man
quite likely of another species
than those of us around him.
Whose condition had no cure.

For my own prayers to be answered,
bombs would have to fall the way
spring snow is falling, unexploded, melting
as they fall, becoming joyful torrents
in a roadside stream.

Missiles and other fire
from shoulder-mounted guns
would strike like seeds and pollen,
wintergreen and broom and helicopter
dragonflies would rise among these rocks and ridges
where the cock and hen grouse eat and drum.

Soldiers, citizens would all go home
to ordinary nightmares and love affairs,
to ordinary deaths.

Jon Mathewson

Walking to Lucy's School

Fermenting strawberries from the Northeast Kingdom
Top off the compost bucket carried in the rain
Out to the garden which pales in comparison
With Sharon's garden, anarchy of greens, flowers
Amongst vegetables, snap peas and pole beans and poppies,
Nasturtium, strawberries, none in rows
Rather by paths which somehow snake their way

From kale to cucumber, forgive the alliteration,
Isn't vacation always like that, comparing gardens,
That which is seen relaxed with what is seen stressed,
And it took about half an hour to walk to Lucy's school,
Another half hour back, finding the final stretch
Having foot deep ruts in the road, the school gone
And Lucy dead and buried in the village graveyard.

At these rutted crossroads in the middle of the forest
We noticed a stonewall, a type usually made by communities,
Not individual farmers, wide at the bottom, narrow
        at the top,
Sturdy, but with the appearance of instability
To confuse the cattle, who steer away from such walls.
None of the other lands had walls, weird for this part
        of the world,
So a century and a half ago, when a hundred and fifty people
        lived here,

With a now vanished school, a recently restored graveyard,
The wall was an act of civic beautification, an attempt
To say, here we are, we are here, this is our village
And now cellar holes dot the half hour walk
Past fields filled with forest back to Sharon's garden,
The house Lucy spent her forty-seven years in,
        which survives
Only because people have repeated, decade after decade,

[more]

We will be here, this is the earth which will nourish us,
And which has ended up nourishing future others.
Relaxed, it is easy to see the continuum. Stressed, and
Out of the continuum, it is a fairy tale,
Easily dismissed and not belonging in this great future.
After dumping the compost bucket, I look around my garden,
And revisualize the real work, what is to be done.

Tim Mayo

The Uncapping

A friend once told me this story
as I was on my way to a wedding.
It happened deep in the woods
on a ridge somewhere west of where
he lived: a woman he once loved
led him there down path after path,
reading signs only she could see,
to show him a secret place in the earth,
shown to her many years before.

It was capped with a nondescript rock
no one would have ever noticed,
which still took all her small weight
to push aside showing the entrance
to an ancient beehive chamber.
Inside: a circular stone wall
rose from the earthen floor, then arced
inward to form a dome making it
seem impossible to scale back up.

He couldn't *believe* they *climbed in*,
so that small opening—its light—
became the only link between them
and the outer world, that they stayed
waiting in the dark, as long as it took,
to see how the buried past hunched
its earth and stone shoulders over them,
and then, they made the difficult
climb out into the rest of their lives.

Partridge Hunting in an Old Orchard
—for Ed Ochester

Day had slumped plumply into sun,
apples fermented on the bough,
and I was logy with it all:

the gold-orange richness of leaves
imbibing the afternoon light,
the sentimental scene I was in

of autumn things in the autumn,
when suddenly my friend shifted,
twisting his body, and fired twice.

I saw two wings rise from a tree
and move away. Then, all at once,
they turned and circled back—all I

had was an upward twitch in time,
faith in someone who knew the woods
better than I—and I shot straight up—

arching back toward what I'd passed,
the whole baggage of my life gathering
in the wake of still air behind me,

and I turned to see the bird's wings fold,
its body fall factual and black.

Jennifer A. McGowan

For Vita, Maybe

I see you leaning against a fence post,
hard and practical, glinting in the light.
You planted the post last spring;
obedient to your will, it grew
and chained this hard soil to your heart, bound it in.
Now when the wind blows your head lifts,
searching the sounds for hidden words,
poems of the old earth and this,
your new home.

Retreat

Moving was a mistake. Now, it's difficult.
This place is as numb as the rest.
Snow hangs thickly to his feet, blankets his head.
"We live down the road a piece," said the nearest,
back when haze rose up in shimmers.
Windows stare blankly. He cannot navigate "a piece";
watches the trees stretch thin and silent shadows.
Stirring, he shivers, hunches shoulders
against his empty eaves. He's sure
there should be swallows, bringing liquid light:
moving words like burgeon and spring, and
young red mouths gaping wide.

Hatsy McGraw

Words I Use for This Green

Chartreuse, celadon, spring, frog,
daffodil stem standing erect
in my side garden, that extra layer
on my skin when it rains, the top
of Bowles Pond after maple sugar season.
Pale, not cedar, not iridescence
on the blackbird's wing. Green
that doesn't yet understand loud, that grows
without restraint not knowing Robin Hood
or teal's mixing with blue. Not that
fearful ocean green, bottomless,
forcing the air out
of my lungs.

Lucretia Went Walking

She paddled down the river in her shoes, naked
except for those. It was the middle of winter.
Purple light, soft on her tongue, she felt
the heat of morning in her thighs. Over Sumner
Falls Lucretia went, walking not floating, moving
slowly nonetheless, good for nothing, slovenly
slut, the dampness caused her hair to grow,
rocks of truth fell at her feet. Along
the murky bottom she ran, big flabby beauty she
was, a river bottom queen. Her flowery knees
were strong as posts. They were the best I'd
ever seen. *Les jeux sont faits* the river whispered
and swallowed hard against her frame. Purple
shoes floated high on foam. End game.

Jeff McRae

Minor Surgery

When we arrive he is very old
and has dropped over the edge
of reverie, out of consciousness,
into dark memory. We come
stamping inside his home
to treat this new problem
with the old tone of knowingness
men who work with their hands
adopt when solving one more
mechanical failure. Sometimes
things wear out. Some things
are broken beyond repair
so then you heft the new axe,
dirty the new shirt, push
the new pen, your favorite tool.
And now, after three by-pass
surgeries, he faces kidney failure
and an undesired life
of dialysis with the next operation.
So there will be no more
surgeries, no more stents
installed, changed out; there are
no more spare solutions.
I want the big one to come
and just end it, Laddie, he says
twisting his hands like he's
breaking a chicken neck.
And so today we gather
around the switch
to the motion-detector light.
He thinks the wiring is bad
or the switch is faulty.

[more]

We stand together, grandfather
and son and grandson,
rain drumming on the tin roof,
passing the switch
back and forth, inspecting
its simple circuitry,
talking-out options: we could
obviously buy a new one.
*No, no need to spend the money
on that*, we're told.
You must acknowledge
concerns of the elders
though they may only
be expressions of fear. So
we remove the switch,
climb in the truck and head
down the rain-ruined drive
to have the wires tested, knowing
he has forgotten to turn on
the outside light.
And when we return
he suspects the fault lies
with himself. We stay for dinner,
talking about family.
After half a dozen games of cribbage
he says, visit again soon.
We walk across the wet yard
and the yellow light blinks
on. I turn as I always do
when leaving, and there he is,
framed in the window, face lost
in shadow, hand raised.

Peter Money

Plume & Climb

Impossible to see
but we knew
what was *there*
was mountain,

is, under a fogged page
so given to being
absent,
allowing us to

live without it
& so we reconcile
our choices & remain
until the vision lifts

or until we intuit
the other
side, until the differences
do not matter.

What Tomorrow Brings

There is a place left in the mind for impression.
Even now, in the rat race, a country mouse finds
a clue, something to sniff out. A squirrel will sort
what's left and the builder will sever the stone
from its rest at the bend of a root.

What falls never fails us. We put to use.
What gives depends. If the offer's true,
we're better from the encounter. What could be
truer than form? I play this game with my children:

"Is it there?" I say about the mountain, disguised in a sheath
of fog. "What happened? Did someone take the top
        of my mountain?"
To this they have learned to say, "No Dad!
        It's there!"—smiling.
"But how do you know it's there?" I demand,
        leading their prompt.

"Because I have seen it so many times" they reply on cue.
I have seen it so many times that the mind harbors
        & the harbor gives:
What the sea turns in, what the moon shadows, what earth
—in all its revolutions—leaves for us. The impression is ours

to waste. But we cannot. We cannot turn our backs
        on our own
curious will to continue and know, to excel and proceed,
to be & to be better. And where our minds slip, fail,
        falter, we rise
up and ask guidance; we seek friendship in understanding

and yet we come out on top, able to breathe &
        share that undivided
yearning. We ascend, commencing, ready for anything.

PAZ.

"Whatever is not stone is light"
and even stone is light in the absence
of hands who weigh them

down, or in earth a bed for
where light was
& warms,

warmed, will
warm again.
Even in hands, especially,

the fingers and the palms of the expired
make a cradle for light;
what was stone was airy also.

We are all the same
with or without,
with *and* without.

Shadow horse on the hillside, neck bowed,
baby bubbling at the mouth on an Afghan rug,
words conflicted and twisted to state—unheard,

here: all down to this
intimate distant goings-on,
not waiting but in motion—

a hunter vexed by anticipated emotion,
a village put to sleep by simple act of night,
a moment of surrender in the serenity of reflection,

a world gone
mad no more than some,
light in the dark—no matter how long, how long.

David Mook

A Vision
—*for Denise Levertov*

Bright eye of morning
blinks for a moment
between the meanwhile veils of passing
clouds.
                    I notice leaves outside
the window, sunlit
emeralds, yellows
never more yellow, themselves like suns,
and the maple's bloody star-shaped leaves hang,
shards of shattered hearts.
                    I watch
the leaves brightening
in the changing
light. I fix my wakeful gaze
on the antique panes. Within
this kaleidoscope, a whim
of startled motion, the unseen
Glazier.

Brenda Nicholson

Ordinary Moon

My friend, Arthur, wants to know why poets
always write about the moon. Tonight,
I set out to prove—it's not always true—

as the full moon became a giant, orange orb,
big as a space ship hovering over Owl's Head Mountain.
I refused to give it a second glance.

But could it be that coyote, howling
in the distance, is really an inconsolable poet,
crying, *moon, moon, you are such a mystery.*

Another Moon

Just as I begin to think there
are no answers for you, for
your life—sullen and calcified—

the full moon begins to rise in the east
large and almost full.

Shining on the snow covered earth, its
misshapen form resembles the bread dough
I placed near the stove in a white glass bowl.

A tenderness rises in me, some
sweetness I surely don't deserve

and I see the world—perfectly imperfect—
and you (and me) piled in its midst—
staggering brilliance, great heaps of shining.

Leslie Paolucci

Peru

We climb through the fence,
struggle through the growth
to the water's edge. The sun shines,
but we are in the shadows
of the trees. We barely speak.
You are a serious twelve-year old
teaching me to fish like Dad
taught you. You remember,
every movement, the way he held
the pole, how he showed you
the deep pools where the rainbows lurk.

But I am eight years old.
I will not sit still.
I fling off my shoes, step
into the cold, dark water, dip
down to find skipping rocks,
scatter fish in my wake.
You look up, unbelieving,
grab my arm and shake me,
shout until I start to cry.

I have broken a rule.
The trout have abandoned
their dark hiding places.
My wet pant-legs cling.
You will not even look at me
as we gather the poles,
as we wade through the deep rippling
grass. I cannot keep up.
You do not notice.
Why won't you stop?
Why can't I find the words
to call you back to me?

Late August

Raspberries fit on the end
of my tongue. I eat them
one by one. My mouth is wet
with summer. Seeds root
in my teeth. Each berry dusty
then dripping warm rain,
like the rain that fell that day
at the Warren parade as we lay
in the field uncaring, as new
to each other as the summer.

I will bring you this
green basket of berries
and feel the wet burst,
the clinging seeds
as you crush them against
the roof of your mouth,
as you reach for another,
never expecting to reach
bottom, not recognizing
the sweet final berry,
unwilling to name it
or the season that follows.

Angela Patten

Thanks for the Genes

Father, it's time I thanked you for
this slender body, its quick metabolism.
Its uncanny knack for fighting off infection.
Its tolerant digestive tract
accommodating as an ash-pit.

I didn't inherit your taste for potatoes
boiled in their jackets, peppery turnips
fried on the pan or two spoons of sugar in your tea.
But thanks to you I can eat
almost anything without remorse.

Forget the delicate fingers, polished nails.
My hands look like yours after a day in the garden
pruning roses and shoveling manure.
Workman's hands, thick fingers.
Veins standing out like the contour lines
on a topographic map of Ireland.

This face you gave me was a tough one
to love, especially now it's turning Cubist
in the mirror, full of jagged planes
and jutting angles, shifting tectonic plates.
Though it does have character
I'll grant you that.

I'm still wrestling with your dagger's looks
your suspicious nature, your moody brooding.
Like Jewelweed, invasive Touch-Me-Not
that sneaks surreptitiously into the flower-bed
just when you think you finally stamped it out.

Signs

Even after I got over all religion
abandoned the very idea of an *Afterlife*
I kept looking for a sign, some
directional signal that would indicate
stay or go, this man or the other.

Like an amputee's limb that continues to agitate
after being severed, I wanted answers
that were clear, unequivocal.
A mathematical equation, a cardinal number.

The answer, it turned out, was more like
one of those infuriating mystery novels
where you get to choose which door
your poor protagonist will open
as he fumbles for the light switch in the dark.

I've never found a sign that wasn't wish-
fulfillment, a mock-up of my own creation.
Like last night driving home I found myself
meandering down a road I'd never seen before.
I had no idea which direction I should take
and for a while I drove as if lifted out of time
cut off from the current of my own existence
no tether tying me to either end.

Exhilarating really to feel so free.

And the sunset, which I hardly ever notice
was spectacular, all reds and purples
deepening to twilight. I passed two horses
cropping late October grass by the roadside
the pond behind them a cup of the light
that tipped their manes and tails with mercury.

But I know better than to call that luminous ploy
a portent, a sign. I've always wondered
if my real life was being lived by some *doppelganger*
on another dimension of Google.com.

Hang out your shingle, they used to say
and mine might well read *Under Construction
Come Back Later, Closed for Repairs.*

Inga M. Potter

Visage

The enormous granite boulder
bears a lichened face, suggesting
furrowed brow and downcast eyes.

Its gray shape rises high above
a sea of windblown steeplechase,
not long ago a meadow, pasture

for a Jersey herd. If this mass
is the head, one ponders on how deep
beneath the earth the torso goes,

how broad the shoulders, vast the chest,
huge the arms and how many meters
to the toes? A continental glacier

that once dressed the east from Labrador
to New Jersey, left souvenirs
of spatial drift. How long this sleep?

How many eons until the cataclysm
of an Appalachian fault shakes Vermont,
freeing this colossus from his ancient vault?

Janice Miller Potter

Potato Paradise

We planted them every spring—
your catalog-ordered Kennebec,
Dark Red Norland, and Cobbler potatoes,
delivered to us in five-pound bags
which you arranged on the cellar floor
beside your three-legged stool.
You, the teacher, preparing potato-heads.
You'd sit for an hour, or more,
nursing each specimen in your hand,
admiring its weight of possibility
before slicing it with your pocket knife
into one-eyed wedges, each one
ready to seek its fortune underground.
We sank them deep and covered them well
with compost and soil and straw mulches
and even shreds of the daily news.

We watched for their sprouts,
beginning with swellings and seams
in the bare earth. Then suddenly—
the revelation of small green fists,
clenched with primal leaves, unfolding.
For you, it seemed a consecration
of some secret pact you'd made
with those potatoes, something you'd
felt for them during the severance
of their wholeness—yes, a promise that
they'd flourish and replenish again.
All summer a tender crown of snow
blossomed over Cobbler and Kennebec,
and over Norland an exotic purple flowering
told us all was well in our potato garden.
And I covered myself in your pleasure.

[more]

One evening, then, when burnt yellow vines
had fallen in tangles upon the ground,
you pulled the fork from where it stood
like a scarecrow among the corn,
and called me to come and to share—
you could not harvest this work alone.
Mapping a circle around a stem,
you plunged sharp tines into the earth
and gently parted its fragrant threads.
Where one potato eye had lain,
now lay a multitude of dusky forms.
So on we fared—with fork and with hands,
exclaiming at our row of new potatoes.
From slivers, I sang the miracle of girth.
But you, with your tenderness for lesser gods,
bade me to gather in the small ones, too.

E. D. Roberts

The Doe

The middle of January and so cold
it brings tears to the eyes. So cold
a television reporter demonstrates
how she can blow frozen soap bubbles
in the air. Just as one floated out of sight, snap,
and the sky turns
a deathly blue. That was the moment ,
one small doe, barely visible from my window,
barely moving, appeared in the woods.
Separated from the herd most likely
in search of food.
The news says large numbers will starve to death
during this unfriendly season. Folks are notified
of their rights—to kill.
We're advised not to offer food; told it's insane to interfere.

Cautiously she considers each step she takes,
just as one would if crossing a mine field.
Reaching the river's edge, she stops, stands in the cold
sunlight sneaking a gray cloak around her shoulders,
eyes wide open. She doesn't move.
She looks like a sculptured figure
in a Masaccio painting: the same tension,
the same energy, her muscles defined—
no doubt her will's as strong and firm as her bones.

She blinks. Even though some distance away,
it's possible to see her eyes sparkle
like the coin St. Peter extracted from the fish's mouth.
Her eyes tax mine until she releases the stare
and starts trudging along her familiar path.
In the open field, her little hooves prance as silent as sanity.

River Voices

In the cloudy spring dawn the snap of ice breaking
Tolls across the Ompompanoosuc.
Along the riverbank and across the field
The sound swells like a flood
Of voices rising from a thousand years
Of heavy sleep, the slow awakening
Emptying out and away until
My thoughts begin to drum
With the ageless voice of wind beating
Upon the windowpanes?
But it's simply the throbbing rhythm
Of eaves dripping that eventually
Overtakes me while I stand
And watch tall hemlocks stretch
Their fingers as if determined
To snatch the music from my soul.
O river, O crier,
Like Proteus I listen to the chorus
Gather strength and scream, "prophesy."
I step away from the window,
And by night the cloudy sky slowly dissolves,
Obtains the stars, and long pools
Of moonlight overrun the riverbanks.

Mark Rubin

Butterfly

Because you will not make it
to Mexico this year or any other, will
no doubt leave the earth as you found it,
in a heartbeat, you notice

a monarch butterfly, the twisted
wing that keeps it earthbound, Zen-like.
You take it home, feed it nectars
of peach and warm watermelon juice

from a spoon, which is what it likes,
though feeding it is more
the need to hear someone say, finally,
You don't have to fly for me. And hearing it

is all about lifting, letting go.
You don't have to fly for me to hold you
on my finger. It dips one foot in then
pulls it out, like doing the hokey-pokey,

and that's what it's all about,
the building of trust, the habit
of walking onto a finger, the safety
of rolling out the tongue, gliding it

under pulp mounds and slippery seeds,
drawing it like a violin bow across
one foot for the sweet, brief taste
of music. This too is what it's about,

the instinct to go on, to lift on three
wings, not four, a night of rest
on a baseboard, a chair leg out
of harm's way. And this too. Soft

light fell across the room and you,
onto your desk, the morning
you crushed it by accident. And this, that
you covered it with a leaf under a bush
whose sweet scent filled the air with burden.

Peggy Sapphire

Afterwards

Look for me in the woods

in old growths of pines

or beneath the last fifty years

of maple leaves   I've made

my peace with rain   frost

my nakedness wears like moss

still sweaty with August sun

September rain   solitary nights

flights of owls   loons skimming

the lake where we floated

by day

you and I

our voices private

hovering with us

I'll be waiting near

maidenhair ferns

but not among them

they are virgins and I

am not   I'll be listening

for leaves beneath your feet.

Hereafter

I've sworn I'll leave this place
when you are gone. Let me be
clear: when I must survive without
you, climb our stairs, walk our
floor, when my hands must close
our front door, or open it with
unnatural hope, they will hold your
hands. When I look up, it will be
as if you reside in the hemlock
beams sanded free of splinters,
chamfered and lamb-tongued. I
will remember wood shavings,
wood-dusting your beard and my
long hair, neither of us able to see
past our glasses. Through the
many windows whose light I had to
have, I'll see our blue spruce,
doubled, even tripled, but never
enough to give shade, another wild
hope. *So what,* we shrugged, *we've
got our old wild apple trees,*
generous with Mac reds each
September, ready for applesaucing,
peel and all, your day of coring,
cutting and stirring, of portioning,
labeling and freezing. In Winter,
the season of water falling like
stones upon my lips, finches &
nuthatches will be longing too,
awaiting your faithful replenishing
of black-oil seeds and suet. I won't
manage their grief and mine.
Upstairs, in the library you
invented, our shelves cut from local
kingdom pine, I would have to face
titles of volumes lugged from
borrowed basements, our former
homes, rented rooms, one last time.

[more]

There will always be mornings of
southeast sun, honey-light in the
afternoons, lupines will seed
themselves, our rosa rugosas will
never need pampering (that was our
plan), lilies on their own, clustered
and weathering with masses of
mallow, daisies and black-eyeds,
our stone path hemmed in every
space by creeping thyme and
myrtle, as if we'd known they'd
also find their way. Best to leave them to their destinies, as I
will be, all promises kept, circles fully
rounded.

Ivy Schweitzer

Snow Day, February 14

Blizzarding outside
and a nipping wind

whips dry powder
into blinding whorls.

I try to will you back to
bed when there's no reason

to leave, but already breakfast
clamors and you are

sunk in routine
tracking yourself through deep

drifts against the danger of going
astray. I try to give you sweetness

you said I used to have before
I gave up seeking danger,

loving to lose sight of
clear paths, craving the pungent

salve we make, hip to hip. I try
to be the flash you live

for in a day crammed with must
do's and have to's, the spicy

bath you slip into sweaty and grateful
after shoveling the roof

where snow has heaped thickly and
falls again, now through your

careful efforts, into higher heaps
blocking the doorway.

Caging the Tulips

Every spring their pale tips
poke through quickening soil
in my neighbor's fussy plot, his perfect
square, five by five,
a tiny platoon of beauty.

I imagine the autumn muster: plump
bulbs with brown papery skins,
bottoms fringed with roots,
roll sleepily from perforated
sacks to be nestled
in close rank and file
precisely eight inches beneath the loam.

In May, showers roust them out,
green recruits of incipient joy.
Sun gives the drill command
and we brace for the cadence
of color—when
the cage
goes up around them.
Four feet of chicken wire
open at the top but tall enough
to deter winter thin deer.

They come, then, smoldering
orange petals with blazing yellow
throats, pitch black at the center,
erect three lobed stigma
ringed by six slender stamen,
their anthers dusty with pollen and curved daintily outward,
splayed cups of exultation
penned in for their own protection.

I lope past
after my morning run,
suddenly remembering how you reached for me
last night, unexpectedly,
how we panted in the dark air suffused by subtle scents
from my rowdy spring beds
laced with manure.

Oh glorious disorder, I croon to the captives,
as if my song could free them.
Let us throw reason to the winds,
let us plant tulips for the spring,
and let ravenous deer
eat the sweet tips—
or not.

Neil Shepard

History Matters More Than You

thought at muscled twenty. Now your body's
soft, growing moss, and so becoming
part of history too like that stunning
monostone across the stream you saw just now
and crossed over and found yourself reduced
by that enormous cliff broken
from some higher place. Perspective shifts
when you're a smaller piece
of the planet. Let the eye travel upward
toward that hilltop flat and peaceful with pines,
and know from some higher precipice once
a piece of rock broke off
and landslid down to this brook's babble
and lodged here until time without chronicler
lapped its sides to shiny skipping pebbles
and what piece was left on shore, a piece
large as a museum, began to house its artifacts
of fox and bear, for their tracks
are still here, and hosted crowds of lichen
and moss upon its roof that broke down
like mortar to pestle the rock to soil and now
a Christian era later hemlock and fir
stand straight and silent as museum guards.
Ask them why this green shade draws the eye
toward its deepest declivities.
Ask them where exactly this trickling stream
issues from, from what higher place the first
rains gathered and carved their rushing course.
Ask in vain how you're part of it,
without name or date, and why this brook will shush
us up who try to ask too much, will lap
instead at our feet and hands, saying skip
this stone across the stream or skip yourself
to the other side.

The Source

Snow deep in north pasture, more
On the way. How odd to read
Her letters, where light lies
Easy on Polynesian waves. She's
There on the quay or under the shade
Of mango and palm, draped in a red
Pareu, listening to the liquid
Sounds of their vowels.
Here, a month of zero
Mercury and words chuffed
In little clouds drifting off
To who knows where.
My brain's split between hemispheres.
Was there ever a year she desired
This house and pasture?
Don't lie. Of course, of course—
And yet—just yesterday
I broke through snow crust
On a downward-sloping field,
Broke through to a deep-running
Spring we'd discovered years ago
When we built here. That gusher
Down in the foundation—we were
Astonished at the water's force.
Half-feared it would obliterate
Concrete, and half-desired it—
Our house balanced on a spume,
A great spinning, shining ride
In the revolving years
Of early love—it almost washed
The backhoe clean as it struck
The source. Later, the force
Lessened to a stream
Manageable and constant.
We diverted it with a simple
Lead pipe out to the field
And forgot about it.
Until now, until I broke through.
Snow falling on my blue parka,

[more]

Blue gloves, blue hat. I know
Where this stream ends –
Where all the springs drain—
Down at the bottom of the pasture
Where birches bend under all this
White weight, and swamp begins.
And nothing but willows grow
In the boggy hummocks, iced up now,
Their roots lifted up
As if trying to take a first, slow step
Out of the rime and ooze. And every living
Thing falls down into the watery spaces
They've abandoned.

On the Occasion of Paul Carriere's Death

(Thanksgiving Day, 1995)

      Inarticulate now as he who disappeared
under the iron back of his tractor.
Hauling logs on a steep Vermont slope,
he rolled under the hard mechanism
of his life's work and lay pinned
by the wheel. I'm making it up
as I go—no neighbor to relay the details—
and without them he's leaving the earth
too soon: firefighters have already levered
the tons of steel from his chest, the ambulance
has already plucked him from November
leaves and mud, cars have carried mourners
to his widow's home beneath the hundred-year cottonwoods,
the adze-planed edges of the closed casket
have been prepared, and the realtor
come with his hammer and sign.

      There has been no time
to fit myself into the proceedings, I who knew him
passably enough to know the depth of our differences
and still to admire the burly, barrel-chested farmer
who brush-hogged my fields and rehearsed the history
of this hilltop. To stand with him and survey
the acres before he mowed them was to prepare
each time for his death. To stand, spit, and talk
across the distances of our chosen lives—
the farmer and the teacher—to hear
in our exchanges the cringing clichés
of two men lost to each other—to hear
yet more than this, some tentative figure
groping along the stonewall of two men's
mental properties and arriving finally at the gap
where the old carriage road once thrived
with farmers, teachers, and all the odd
figures of the community, and take it back
to the 1940s when Paul Carriere farmed alone
on this hillside, fashioned a rope-tow

[more]

during mudseason to skim his milkjugs
down to the village. And back further
to the first plot-owners of the 1840s
who planted cottonwoods, raised the house,
trees and house growing together, the house
doubling, doubling again as generations
of farmers milked, hayed, froze, and endured.

        Until Paul bought the farm in '45,
farmed, froze, fell, and rose up again, time
after time, herd after herd, until time passed him by
for good at the swishing tail-end of the century,
and he joined the farming legions going under.
Then rose again and turned his hand to even smaller-
scale miracles of survival, carpentry, logging,
fieldwork, and talking, delivering our firewood,
hammering our homes, rehearsing, reharrowing
the local hilltop history … until this Thanksgiving
when the iron machine reared up and crushed him,
and his moment of going

        is upon us, where I've tried to hold him
before he vanishes into history, into the hillside
cemetery beneath the chiseled stones, or crosses
the sidereal isthmus, the blueblack azimuth
to the place I've always imagined beyond imagining,
where he can perch on the crown of those hundred-year
cottonwoods, sing for all he was worth,
and I can let him go.

Monica Stillman

Traveling

At first I was small, unfurling
in the shade of a thousand leaves;
a club moss, or a seedling
in need of a clearing

In surpassing disappointments
I grew into a mountain
bold and sure
shouldering storms

When those strengths failed me
I turned to running water
carrying only what I needed
traveling on

Today I hover between landscapes
neither bowing nor exalted
Queen Anne's lace in summer breeze
awaiting what comes next

Joyce Thomas

Martha

> *"Lost: Brazilian arboreal parrot, green with red markings.*
> *Tame, talks some, answers to Martha.*
> *Last seen near S. Ellis Orchard Rd."*
>
> Notice posted in the E-Z
> Wash, Castleton Corners

One thinks of cracker-loving Pollies trained to ride
    teeny tricycles
or sit in rows and dingle bells, heads bobbing,
claws raised as if to wave hello.
Of Long John's Captain Flint,
pieces of eight threading the Vermont maples,
fifteen men on the dead man's chest spooking the grazing cows.
Of Monty Python's defunct avian being rapped on
    the counter like a cane,
the bird that irrefutably has ceased.

But it is November, men, guns and beer about to claim
    our woods,
and the parrot Martha lost in the cold, winging alien
as King Kong in snowy Manhattan.

Standing in the Laundromat with my sheets, I cannot help
thinking of the parrot lost among the conifers
awaiting her dish of seeds,
and of the cage that sits empty, its wire door swung open
like a plea, *come home.*
What words, I wonder, have they taught her,
what words that can save?

Martha, it is getting late.
Can you not see, O, Martha, the horned shadow
about to drop like night's cloth?

The moose stops time

While the man in the flatbed truck parks
and reads his morning paper, moose materializes
on the other side of Drake Road
strolling toward the meadow
as if he had all
the time in the world

while I, walking the dog, watch him
cross over the newly laid asphalt, saunter
through the cricket grasses, dimming
August flowers and fuzz,
thistle downy muzzle snuffing the air
perhaps to breathe me
and the dog who only has nose
for what cousin has passed,
pissed near its paws

not this implausible masked horse
moving past snapped saplings,
flattened weeds that track a yellow bulldozer
beside whose sleeping caterpillar
he stops

looks upon the woods,
the field below, excavation's
earthly heaps, the black scythe of road
where dog and woman stand
for all eternity

or until golden
rod, asters part, tree-
crowned moose walks

and the man in the flatbed truck checks his watch,
turns the page.

Skins

The thing protrudes from the stacked slate steps of the house
like the stones' own slack tongue, old
cellophane casing flagging its past, checker-
stamped on this shucked wrapper
crinkling to the fire of my finger-
tip's touch as if

to contract farther in the fissure
where, once on a near time, wedged adder
heaved,
       huffed,
             unzippered itself—
                       cast off

the worn envelope of scales
and, newly nude,
left rebirth's caul behind

      like those crusts of summer cicadas
      one sometimes finds
      clinging to the bark like tiny Tutankhamens
      and just as much a marvel
      to behold their light
      as dust, bug-eyed rinds,
      cradle in the palm
      the winged, clawed transparencies
      that yet can scratch you into bleeding
      as if alive

so his filmy peel alongside my own
habitation gives pause

serves to remind he was here and had been
in the shadows always, this hiss-
less husk of
serpent that is not
emptied wholly

Susan Thomas

Ennis Hill Road

I know this road like the back of my hand.
Here is my life line: the place
I jumped a snow bank when
my neighbor's daughter's boyfriend's car
slid on black ice and I landed
in a small ravine. The car
came to rest on my footprints.

Here is my love line: the place
we walked to the day we broke up.
We stopped at the dip in the road to argue
and moved in together instead.

We walk this road at bedtime,
discussing constellations, getting
the stars mixed-up: Deneb, Spica,
Arcturus, Capella. We gasp
as things fall out of the sky, leaving
sparks in their place for a while.

This is the road we know is home,
the road we navigate each day.
Our bodies hold its ups and downs.
Its curves know how to ride us.
We've learned its tricks and turns by heart,
its blind spots, wash-outs, straightaways.
We love the way it dances the ridge,
drops into the valley, singing.

Windowlight Supper
—after Pavese

The disappearing sky has thrown blue all
over the uplands. The hills are blue, the fields,
even the cows and the trees behind them.
I can still pick out twigs and the frozen

apples clinging to their fingers. Deer float up
in the blue, not quite invisible, watching me watch
them eat the frozen apples while I pick at what's left
of my dinner. I can still make out the food

on my plate, blue tomatoes, blue rice, blue onions.
Soon the stars will fling themselves into darkness.
Nothing ever stops. Time makes no difference.
It circles overhead, watching me. I swallow

my dinner and listen to the clatter of plants
and seasons. I stand at the window, envying
the stars for their chummy ways with each other,
for the brilliant lives they lead in the frozen

throat of the cosmos while I hold fast
the warm house, this room with chairs and books
and table holding food I planted last year in
the tipped bowl of garden under this window.

Lynn Valente

Rural Essay

He is with us on furlough from a flat
bleached, hard place. "But
don't you get blind sometimes
to beauty?" The starving man
doesn't want to lose his craving
for food.

Listen, mountains seem like food
only until you say
I live here. Then they keep feeding you
the way air feeds you. You don't
consume this place. Think of marriage
to a person with a beautiful face.
His beauty will continue to strike you
often, at odd times, but

if you're to have a life together,
you can't stand around and gape
in wonder more than a few hundred
times a day.

Dianalee Velie

Maple

A seedling burst into life,
trapped in the tiny fissure of a boulder,
every year widening that crack
until completely severing the granite,
conquering stone with steady sweetness.

No violence tore the rock apart,
only slow insistent force and time.
But now the big maple is down.
The six sap buckets, once
clinging to her like children,

brimming with her collected
nectar, lay orphaned
in the sugar-lot, where I stop
in my snowshoes, suddenly
aching for my mother.

The matriarch has relinquished
her throne. Her massive crown
lies fallen beneath the snow.
Her trunk displays
hundreds of tap holes

drilled into her solid body,
possibly hastening her demise.
Bowed down to wind and time,
she will leave only this cracked
rock, as a lasting sign

of her strength, but my splintered
heart will memorize this moment,
knowing neither time nor chain saw
can disturb deeply planted roots.

Simon Walsh

Vermont Life

One evening , you're home from work, stiff and tired
    from city life
looking over the wife's shoulder at real estate on the internet ;
next thing you know you're living in a parallelogram
'in need of your creative touch,' 150 miles from
    inner-city gentrification
and the last of those sun-dried Portuguese underpants—
and the first thing she seeks out is the town dump.

So you crawl out and dust yourself down and
leave her with everything except the dog on weekends.
The realtor she's been knocking around with helps you
get fixed up with a part-insulated chicken shed
at the top of a winding ribbon of ice
where one of those gear-jamming logging trucks
has your name written backwards on the grill in blood.

First winter, you stuff the wood stove
with gleanings of beaver lodge and unopened legal bills,
and you boost the circulation of the Free Weekly Shopper
by the armload (dampened for a slow burn).
An 'all-nighter' used to be a good party
But now you know it's a big fat log.
The thermometer needs your viagra more than you—
it's you or winter, whoever blinks first
and like the Renaissance Man you think about becoming
you go to bed with your clothes on.

Then one day steam starts rising from the forest,
the snowplows are drowsing idly among the wildflowers,
so you're outside frantically planting anything that has a
growing season so short
it would take you longer to incubate rabies—
meanwhile, you're already sizing up old man winter again
who is happily stretched out sunning himself
where your woodpile ought to be.

Kimberly Ward

Hurricane in Vermont

After the hurricane, we went out to help our neighbors.
In the dawn, the moon was just a sliver, sharp and small.
The cows beneath the barn called out like an anguished
village
and were silenced with each successive blow from Daddy's
shotgun.

Harvest Time

Red moon this morning.
I am walking barefoot
in puddles and find
the hogs have been killed
uphill.

Constance West

Turtle Ranching

Moved to the hills a while back,
thought I could do that Nearing thing,
you know, living on the land,

eat what you grow, grow what you eat,
you know, that really healthy stuff,
chard, kale, beans, all that hearty stuff when the frost
comes early and stays late.
Tried potatoes, but I couldn't tell the potatoes
    from the stones,
and I grew more stones than potatoes.
Stones make mighty poor eating in the wintertime.

I dug my garden in the spring, down in the bottomland
near the river. Should be rich soil,
I said. Planted up rows of carrots, beans, beets, onions,
and waited. And I waited, and I waited.
And I looked, and said now, didn't I do this just
like Helen and Scott? But nothing
came up. Nothing at all.

By July I'd given up on my garden.
And then it came, turtles, lots of baby turtles
coming out of my garden, each the size of a 50¢ piece.
I was a turtle farmer, I could fence them and ranch turtles,
round them up in the springtime, herd them out on my range.
And here I'd be at the Farmers' Market under my sign
"Free Range Turtles."

Neal Whitman

Behind the Lye Brook Falls

a small slate-gray bird

leaps into the pool

flies onto a floating log

and gobbles an aquatic insect

grabbed when underwater

accompanied by water trill

it tips its head back

and sings a water song

while bobbing up and down

peee peee pijur pijur

it submerges again

and taking its squirming prize

flies though the falls—

sans shoes and socks

I wade my way into its water cave

there with an arched opening

a domed nest of soft green moss—

two baby water birds

singing a water song learned

before they were born

Biographies

Pamela Ahlen from Woodstock, Vt., was Program Director for Woodstock's Third Annual Bookstock, a Festival of Words. She is an avid skier and hiker and "end to ender" of Vermont's Long Trail. Recent poems have appeared in *Main Street Rag*, *Bloodroot*, and *Cider Press Review.*

Ben Aleshire grew up in Wallingford, and is now based in Burlington. His poems have appeared in *Poetry East, Barrow Street,* and others. He was recently awarded a grant from the Vermont Arts Council, and this summer he will be in residence at the BCA Center. Ben edits *The Salon*; his first book, *Dropped Apples,* will be released this summer.

Stuart Bartow teaches writing and literature at SUNY Adirondack. His collection, *Reasons to Hate the Sky,* was published by WordTech Editions, which also published his collection, *Questions for the Sphinx,* in 2011. Chair of the Battenkill Conservancy, a grassroots environmental group, he tries to spend as much time as possible in the summer fly fishing in streams around the New York-Vermont border not far from his home in Salem, N.Y.

Jeff Bernstein is a lifelong New Englander, writer, and energy lawyer who divides his time between Boston and Central Vermont. Poetry is his favorite and earliest art form (he can't draw a whit or hold a tune). His chapbook, *Interior Music,* was published by Foothills Publishing in 2010. Jeff's writer's blog is hurricanelodge.com.

Partridge Boswell, from Woodstock, is founder of Bookstock: The Green Mountain Festival of Words, and managing editor of Harbor Mountain Press based in White River Junction. Singer/ lyricist, and poet, he has performed widely. His poems have recently appeared in *the minnesota review, Rattle, The Literary Review, New Delta Review,* and in his chapbook *In Hindsight, a Happy Accident.*

Regina Murray Brault has twice been nominated for the Pushcart Prize. Her awards include: 2007 Euphoria and Skysaje Enterprises Poetry Competitions, and the 2008 Creekwalker Prize. Regina's poems have appeared in more than 130 different magazines, anthologies, chapbooks, journals and newspapers.

T. Alan Broughton lives in Burlington, Vt. A recipient of a Guggenheim Fellowship and NEA Award, he has published novels, poems and stories. His most recent books are his seventh collection of poems, *A World Remembered* (Carnegie Mellon

University Press, 2010), and short stories, *Suicidal Tendencies* (Colorado State University Press, 2003).

Joseph Bruchac lives in Greenfield Center, N.Y., in the same house where he was raised by his grandparents. There, he and his late wife Carol founded *The Greenfield Review Press*. His poems and stories, which often reflect his Abenaki ancestry, have appeared in many magazines and anthologies.

Judith Chalmer wants to walk into her 60's with open eyes, hand in hand with her partner, Lisa. Chalmer is co-translator of *Deepening Snow*, a collection of haiku and tanka with author Michiko Oishi (Plowboy Press, 2012). She finds enormous pleasure in the work of VSA Vermont, a nonprofit devoted to arts and disability, of which she is Director.

Anna Chapman grew up in Alaska and has lived most of her adult life in New Hampshire and Vermont. She is a freelance editor specializing in medical journals. Her poems have been published in *Yankee* and *Explorations*.

Elayne Clift is a writer, journalist, workshop leader, and lecturer from Saxtons River, Vt. Her work in a variety of genres has been widely published internationally. In January her first novel, *Hester's Daughters,* was published by OGN Publications.

Carol Cone, a retired teacher and administrator from The Dalton School in New York City, is a *Birchsong* editor. Since 1990 she and her husband, Eric, have lived in Dorset, Vt., where she writes with the Northshire Poets. She also writes short stories and has written four novels with the National Novel Writers Month challenge. One of her poems was selected for Poetry Alive 2011 in Montpelier.

Greg Delanty's *Collected Poems 1986–2006* is out from the Oxford Poet's series of Carcanet Press. Other books include *The Word Exchange, Anglo-Saxon Poems in Translation* (W. W. Norton, 2010), *The Ship of Birth* (Carcanet Press, Louisiana State University Press, 2006), *The Blind Stitch* (Carcanet Press, LSU Press, 2003), and *The Hellbox* (Oxford University Press, 1998). Recipient of a Guggenheim for poetry, he is Artist in Residence at Saint Michael's College and recent past president of The Association of Literary Scholars, Critics, and Writers (ALSCW).

Arlene Distler, a freelance journalist on the arts for regional and national publications, lives and works in the Brattleboro area. She is co-founder of Write Action, a not-for-profit writers' organization for southeastern Vermont. Her poetry has been published in several journals including *Kalliope, North American Review, Chrysalis Reader, New Millennium Writings,* and on-line in *Raving Dove.*

Danny Dover is a piano technician who has lived in an old school house in Bethel, Vt., with his wife, Mary, since 1978. His poems have been published in the 2009, 2010, 2011, and 2012 editions of *Bloodroot Literary Magazine.* He has one published book of poems, *Thankful Soup, Kindness Tea* (Dhotarap Press, 2005), available through the author (tashidelek@comcast.net).

George Drew was born in Mississippi and now lives in New York State. He is the author of four collections of poetry. *American Cool,* his third collection, won the 2010 Adirondack Literary Award for best poetry book of 2009. His fourth, *The View from Jackass Hill* (Texas Review Press, 2011) won the 2010 X.J. Kennedy Poetry Prize.

Linda Durkee, an artist, photographer, and writer, lives and works in Danby, Vt. She has had careers as a teacher; journalist in Washington, DC; speechwriter at the U.S. Environmental Protection Agency; and communications advisor at the U.N. Environment Program in Geneva, Switzerland. Her poetry has been published in *Poet Lore, National English Journal,* and *Wisconsin Review.*

Florence Fogelin's poem, "Finale," was included in Poetry Alive 2011 in Montpelier. Redgreene Press published her chapbook, *Facing the Light,* in 2001. Her poetry has appeared in *Negative Capability, Poet Lore,* and the *Cumberland Poetry Review.* A resident of White River Junction, she spends portions of the year in Littleton, N.H., New York City, and Italy.

Lené Gary lives in Montpelier, Vt., and holds an MFA from Vermont College of Fine Arts. She has won national literary awards for her poetry and essays. When she's not writing, you can find her paddling her well-worn Mad River canoe.

Alice Wolf Gilborn is publisher and editor of *Birchsong* and is founder of *Blueline* (SUNY Potsdam, N.Y.) and The Blueline Press (Danby, Vt.). A writer and book editor, her nonfiction book, *What Do You Do With a Kinkajou?* (Lippincott) will be reprinted this year by The Blueline Press. A chapbook, "Taking Root," is forthcoming from Finishing Line Press, and Adirondack essays from Potsdam College Press.

Kirk Glaser's poetry has appeared in *The Threepenny Review, Cerise Press, Sou'wester, Bloodroot Literary Magazine,* and elsewhere. His poetry has been nominated twice for the Pushcart Prize and won numerous awards. He teaches writing at Santa Clara University, where he serves as faculty advisor to the *Santa Clara Review*, and is co-editor of the annual anthology, *New California Writing* (Heyday Press).

Barry Goldensohn is the author of six books of poems; the most recent is *The Listener Aspires to the Condition of Music* from Fomite Press.

Jack Gundy is a retired pediatrician who lives in Corinth, Vt., with his wife Sally and daughter Josie. He studied poetry with Richard Eberhardt at Dartmouth, and has attended several poetry workshops at the Frost Place in Franconia N.H.; and with April Ossmann at the Writing Center in White River Junction, Vt. His poems have been published in *Bloodroot Literary Magazine*, *The Edison Literary Review*, and the Town of Corinth Annual Reports.

Kathleen McKinley Harris, from Charlotte, Vt., has published poems in *Snowy Egret*, *Blueline*, *Sow's Ear*, *Vermont Life*, and June Cotner's anthology, *Animal Blessings*. Morrow Jr. published her children's book, *The Wonderful Hay Tumble*. She was co-editor and co-owner of the paper, *The Champlain Courier*. She currently copyedits Vermont Farm Bureau's quarterly, *Fences*.

Betsy Byrne Hubner, *Birchsong* artist, has an MFA from the Art Institute of Boston at Lesley University and has taught at Burr and Burton academy since her move to Vermont in 1988. Inspired by Vermont's surroundings and its wild and domestic animals, her colorful acrylic paintings, exhibited extensively throughout New England, have won statewide acclaim. She is also a professor at Castleton State College and is distinguished as Vermont's first National Board Certified teacher involved in setting national standards for what art teachers need to know and be able to do.

David Huddle, currently Distinguished Visiting Professor of Creative Writing at Hollins University, is finishing his thirtieth summer as a faculty member of the Bread Loaf School of English. His third novel, *Nothing Can Make Me Do This*, was published by Tupelo Press last October, and his seventh poetry collection, *Black Snake at the Family Reunion*, will appear from LSU Press in 2012. He retired from UVM in 2009 and lives in Burlington with his wife, Lindsey, and his daughter Bess and her husband Nick, not far from his other daughter Molly and her husband Ray.

Rob Hunter is *Birchsong's* guest editor. His first volume of poetry, *September Swim*, was published by Spoon River Poetry Press in 2005.

Since then he has been writing fiction, screenplays, and one act plays. He teaches English at Burr and Burton Academy in Manchester, Vt.

Greg Joly homesteads in the Maynard Hollow valley of Jamaica, Vt., which is still unearthing itself from TS Irene's August floods. When not cutting firewood, hauling rocks, setting type, editing various manuscripts for others, canning the garden harvest or wrestling a snowblower down a 1200-foot dirt driveway, he may find the time (if not the energy) to write.

Phyllis Beck Katz lives in Norwich, Vt., and teaches at Dartmouth College. She has published poems in a number of journals, including, *The Connecticut River Review,* 2008, *Ekphrasis,* 2009, *The* Salon, 2010, and *Bloodroot Literary Magazine* 2010, 2011, 2012. She was nominated for a Pushcart Prize in 2010. Her first book, *All Roads Go Where They Will,* was published by Antrim House Books in December 2010.

Jean L. Kreiling teaches music at Bridgewater State University in Massachusetts. Her poetry has appeared in numerous print and on-line literary journals, and she has been a finalist for the *Dogwood* Poetry Prize, the Frost Farm Prize, and the Howard Nemerov Sonnet Award. Her interdisciplinary essays on music and poetry have been published in several academic journals.

Lyn Lifshin has published over 120 books and edited four anthologies. Recent books include: *The Licorice Daughter, My Year with Ruffian* (Texas Review Press), *Another Woman Who Looks Like Me* (Black Sparrow at Godine, following *Cold Comfort* and *Before It's Light*). Also, *Persephone, Barbaro, Katrina, Ballroom,* and *All the Poets Who Have Touched Me.*lynlifshin.com.

Daniel Lusk is author of *Lake Studies: Meditations on Lake Champlain* (LCMM, 2011), *Kissing the Ground: New & Selected Poems* (Onion River, 1999), and other books. His poems have appeared in *Poetry, New Letters, Prairie Schooner, The Iowa Review, American Poetry Review, North American Review, Nimrod, The Southern Review,* and many other literary journals. He teaches poetry and creative writing at the University of Vermont.

Jon Mathewson is a curator by day and a poet by night. His most recent collection, *While Strangers Insult the Decor,* was released by Foothills Publishing in 2011. He lives in Middletown Springs with his wife, children, cats, and bees.

Tim Mayo's work appeared in *Poetry International, Poet Lore, Verse Daily, Web Del Sol Review of Books, The Writer's Almanac,* and many other places. His collection, *The Kingdom of Possibilities,* was published in 2009. He lives in Brattleboro, Vt., where he is on the Author Committee for the Brattleboro Literary Festival.

Jennifer A. McGowan, a disabled poet, was mostly raised in New England (including some years in Vermont), and now lives near Oxford in the UK. She has published poetry in many prominent magazines on both sides of the Atlantic, and her chapbook, *Life in Captivity,* is available from Finishing Line Press in the U.S. She has also published prose and both written and recorded songs. She holds a PhD in English. jenniferamcgownan.com.

Hatsy McGraw has written poetry for more than twenty years and has published in several literary magazines including *Bloodroot, Hanging Loose, The Salon,* and *Across Borders.* In 2005 she graduated from Vermont College's Writing for Children/YA program. She and her husband, painter Tom McGraw, live in Hartland, Vt. She has been Library Director and Children's Librarian at various Upper Valley libraries and is currently employed as the Library Media Generalist at the Bernice A. Ray School in Hanover, N.H.

Jeff McRae is an adjunct English professor at Massachusetts College of Liberal Arts in North Adams, Mass. He earned an MA in Writing from the University of New Hampshire and an MFA in Poetry from Washington University in St. Louis. His poems have most recently appeared in *The Mind's Eye, The Beloit Poetry Review,* and *The Cimmeron Review.* He lives in North Bennington with his wife, artist Erin McKenny, and their two sons, Finn and Charlie.

Peter Money's poems have appeared in *The Sun, The American Poetry Review,* in the City Lights anthology *Days I Moved Through Ordinary Sound,* and on Garrison Keillor's "The Writer's Almanac." His books include the poetry hybrids *Che.: A Novella in Three Parts, To day -- Minutes only,* and the poetry/music collaboration *Blue Square* (Pax Recordings, distributed by Tupelo Press). His other printed collections include *These Are My Shoes, Finding It, Instruments, Between Ourselves,* and translations (with Sinan Antoon) of the Arab Modernist Saadi Youssef's new poems (Graywolf Press).

David Mook began writing poetry after the sudden death of his eight-year-old daughter Sarah, a poet who started composing poems in kindergarten. His book, *Each Leaf,* includes Sarah's poems. For David, poetry is both a life-changing and life-affirming gift from Sarah. The *Sarah Mook Poetry Prize,* an annual contest for students in grades K-12, seeks to encourage young writers and to honor Sarah's gift of poetry. David has an MFA in Writing from Vermont College.

Brenda Nicholson is a founding member of the Northshire Poets writing group and is a *Birchsong* editor. Her love of poetry has taken her around the world, from Mallorca to Slovenia, to study and work with poets. She has worked with many exceptional mentors, and is especially grateful to Patricia Fargnoli, Ellen Bass, and Jen Bervin. She has an MFA in poetry from Vermont College of Fine Arts.

Leslie Paolucci lives in Shaftsbury, Vt., with her husband and her daughter. She is a graduate of Goddard College with an MFA in Creative Writing. Her poems have appeared in *Cafe Review, Thirteenth Moon,* and *Yankee Magazine,* as well as other publications.

Angela Patten is author of two poetry collections, *Reliquaries* and *Still Listening,* both from Salmon Poetry, Ireland. Her poems have appeared in many literary journals including *The Literary Review, Prairie Schooner, Michigan Quarterly Review, Poetry Ireland Review;* and in anthologies including *Cudovista Usta (Marvellous Mouth)* Slovenia, and *The White Page/An Bhileog Bhan: Twentieth Century Irish Women Poets.* Born and raised in Dublin, Ireland, she now teaches at the University of Vermont.

Inga M. Potter's work has appeared in *The Mountain Troubadour,* chapbook of The Poetry Society of Vermont. She is an artist as well as a poet, painting in oils and acrylics, especially portraits, and exhibits in "The Vermont Festival of the Arts" Big Round Barn Art Show yearly. From Waitsfield, she and her husband, Olin, have lived in Vermont for more than 40 years.

Janice Miller Potter is the author of *Psalms in Time* (Finishing Line Press, 2008) and the recipient of the Sara Henderson Hay Prize for Poetry in 2005. Her poetry has appeared in *Poet Lore, Connecticut Review, The Worcester Review* and elsewhere. She lives in Cornwall, Vt.

E. D. Roberts is a Pushcart Prize nominee. Her poetry has appeared in numerous literary publications. Awards for her work include a Chester H. Jones National Poetry Prize and a New England Writers Poetry Prize. She is the co-founder and the Editor of *Bloodroot Literary Magazine.* She lives in Thetford Center, Vt.

Mark Rubin's poems have appeared in *Crazyhorse, The Gettysburg Review, The Ohio Review, The Virginia Quarterly Review,* and elsewhere. A past recipient of the Discovery/*The Nation* Award and a National Endowment for the Arts Grant, his first book of poems, *The*

Beginning of Responsibility, was published by Owl Creek Press (1992). He is a psychotherapist in private practice in Burlington, Vt.

Peggy Sapphire's poetry appears in various anthologies, including *Poets Against The War*, *Hurricane Blues: Stories about Katrina & Rita*. She has two poetry collections, *Possible Explanations* (Partisan Press, 2006) and *In The End A Circle* (Antrim House, 2009). She is former editor of *Connecticut River Reivew*, former member of the Frost Place Board of Trustees, Franconia, N.H., and a recipient of a Vermont Studio Center Fellowship, 2010. She and her husband live in the Northeast Kingdom of Vermont.

Ivy Schweitzer is Professor of English and Women's and Gender Studies at Dartmouth College. She has published in Dartmouth's literary magazines, two "Anthologies" from the Frost Place's Festival of Poetry, and *Bloodroot Literary Magazine*. She lives in Norwich, Vt.

Neil Shepard published two new books in 2011: a full book of poems, *(T)ravel/Un(t)ravel* (Mid-List Press), and a chapbook, *Vermont Exit Ramps* (Pudding House Press). He taught for many years in the BFA Writing Program at Johnson State College (Vt.) and now teaches in the low-residency MFA program at Wilkes University (Pennsylvania). He is the founder and senior editor of the literary magazine, *Green Mountains Review*.

Monica Stillman, a *Birchsong* editor, is an environmental scientist who relocated to Vermont four years ago to get back to the mountains following too many years of suburban life. She is greatly enjoying the opportunity to be part of her local poetry group. Her poem "Passage" appears in the 2011 edition of *Blueline*.

Joyce Thomas, a professor of English at Castleton College, Vermont, is the author of one non-fiction work, *Inside the Wolf's Belly: Aspects of the Fairy Tale*, and one collection of poetry, *Skins*. Currently she is working on a collection of short stories.

Susan Thomas' collection, *State of Blessed Gluttony* (Red Hen Press), won the Benjamin Saltman Prize. *Last Voyage: Selected Poems of Giovanni Pascoli* (Red Hen Press), was co-translated with Richard Jackson and Deborah Brown. *The Empty Notebook Interrogates Itself* has just been published by Fomite Press. She lives in Marshfield, Vt., and New York City. susanthomas1.com.

Lynn Valente is a retired Vermont high-school Spanish teacher, enjoying a return to earlier interests in music and poetry. She is at work on her first chapbook, *Early Riser*. She also likes to hike, ski, and travel. She lives with her husband near Brattleboro, Vt.

Dianalee Velie lives and writes in Newbury, N.H. She is a graduate of Sarah Lawrence College and has a Master of Arts in Writing from Manhattanville College. She is the author of three books of poetry, *Glass House, First Edition,* and *The Many Roads to Paradise*, published by Rock Village Publishing in Middleborough, Mass.; and a collection of short stories, *Soul Proprietorship: Women in Search of Their Souls,* published by Plain View Press in Austin, Tex. dianaleevelie.com.

Simon Walsh lives in Brattleboro, Vt. He teaches English at Greenfield Community College and works for a hunger relief agency in Cambridge, Mass. His poems have been published in *Willow Springs, The Watermark, The Manchester Literary Journal* and in 2011 in the window of a well-known hardware retailer in Montpelier.

Kimberly Ward received her MFA in Performance Poetry from Goddard College in 1998. Her poetry has been published in the *Green Mountains Review, Vermont Times, Circumference*, and *Metropolis*. Her poetic play "Light" was produced by MOXIE Productions in 2009. She is the founder and president of The Vermont Playwrights Circle. She lives in Montpelier, Vt.

Constance West lives in Manchester, Vt., with her husband. She has lived in Vermont for almost 30 years, raised two children, and worked as associate editor of the journal, *The Review of Archaeology*.

Neal Whitman was born in Boston and headed west, first through Framingham, and then by way of New York, Ann Arbor, Chicago, and Salt Lake City. Today he resides in Pacific Grove, Calif., where he tootles around town in a little white hatchback with the auto plate PG POET in a frame inscribed "Poetic License." Neal is a member of the New England Poetry Club and has published in *Vermont Literary Review, Common Ground Review,* and *Aurorean* among other journals. He and his wife, Elaine, are co-creators of many published haiga: her photographs paired with his haiku.

Credits

Permission to reprint previously published work in *Birchsong* has been granted by the authors. We are grateful to the publications and presses listed below for the opportunity to reprint work by the following poets:

Pamela Ahlen: "Lawn Party" appeared as a part of "Poetry Alive" in Montpelier.

Partridge Boswell: "Just Remember I Knew You When" first appeared in *Main Street Rag* and later in the chapbook *In Hindsight, a Happy Accident* (Pudding House, 2008).

Regina Murray Brault: "Mother Tongue" was previously published in June Cotner's 1999 Random House Anthology, *Mothers and Daughters*.

Elayne Clift: "Signs of Vermont" first appeared in *Love Letters to Vermont: A New England Journal* (OGN, 2001) and is reprinted here by permission of the author.

Greg Delanty: "Driving in Vermont" first appeared in his *Collected Poems 1998–2006* (England: Oxford Poets series of Carcanet Press, 1986).

Arlene Distler: "The Case Against Mums" was published in *A Chrysalis Reader, Kaleidoscope: Lenses On Reality* (Swendenborg Foundation Press, 2010) and *The Best of Write Action, No. 2: The Tenth Anniversary Anthology* (Small Pond Press, 2010).

George Drew: "Elegy for Jarad" appeared originally in *The Journal of Kentucky Studies*. "Instructions for Sitting on the Famous Poet's Porch" first appeared in *Blueline*.

Kirk Glaser: "Element of May" was published in *The Aurorean* 26, no. 1 (Spring/Summer, 2011).

Rob Hunter : "September Swim" is from *September Swim* (Spoon River Poetry Press, 2005).

Greg Joly: "Town Meeting" is from *Village Limits* (Adastra Press, 2008).

Daniel Lusk: "Bull on the Roof" first appeared in *New Letters*.

Tim Mayo: "The Uncapping" first appeared in *Verse Wisconsin,* Issue 102. "Partridge Hunting in an Old Orchard" first appeared in *The Equinox* and also appears in *The Kingdom of Possibilities* (Mayapple Press, 2009).

Jennifer A. McGowan: "For Vita, Maybe" was published in the 2010 volume of the *Vermont Literary Review*. "Retreat" was published in the 2011 volume of the *Vermont Literary Review*.

Hatsy McGraw: "Lucretia Went Walking" was first published, in an earlier version, in *Word Riot* (August, 2009).

Peter Money: "Plume & Climb" appeared in *Rivendell*'s "North of Boston" issue (Sebastian Matthews, editor). "What Tomorrow Brings" was first read next to former U.S. Surgeon General C. Everett Koop at a public event in Lebanon, N.H. "PAZ." first appeared in *Art/Life: The Original Limited Edition Monthly*, Ventura, Calif.

Leslie Paolucci: "Peru" was published under the title "Fishing" in the Fall 1995 issue of *The Cafe Review*.

Inga M. Potter: "Visage" was previously published in *The Mountain Troubadour*.

E. D. Roberts: "The Doe" was winner of the Chester H. Jones Prize.

Mark Rubin: "Butterfly" was originally published in *Crazyhorse*, no. 58.

Peggy Sapphire: "Hereafter" and "Afterwards" first appeared in her book, *In The End A Circle* (Antrim House, 2009).

Ivy Schweitzer: "Snow Day, February 14" was published in *Bloodroot Literary Magazine* 2 (2009); "Caging the Tulips" was published in *Bloodroot Literary Magazine* 4 (2011).

Neil Shepard: "History Matters More Than You," "On the Occasion of Paul Carriere's Death," and "The Source" all appear in his third book, *This Far from the Source* (Mid-List Press, 2006).

Joyce Thomas: "Skins," and "The moose stops time," 1999 National Poetry Competition commendation, Chester H. Jones Foundation, were published in Joyce Thomas, *Skins: Poems* (Fithian Press, 2001). "Martha" first appeared in *Blueline* 31 (2010).

Susan Thomas: "Ennis Hill Road" was first published by *Sun Dog* (Fall, 1999). "Windowlight Supper" was first published by *Notre Dame Review* (Summer, 2003).

Lynn Valente: "Rural Essay" was published in *Heartbeat of New England : An Anthology of Contemporary Nature Poetry*, James Fowler, ed. (Tiger Moon Productions, 2000).

Dianalee Velie: "Maple" was first published in *Northwoods Journal* (2001).